Through the Cellar Door

Through the Cellar Door

Australia's beautiful wineries and vineyards, their design and architecture

For my husband John.

Thank you for your support, encouragement and the wine.

Contents

8   Australian winery architecture and design

South Australia

McLaren Vale
- 12   d'Arenberg Cube
- 18   Beresford
- 26   Dowie Doole
- 32   Mitolo
- 40   Primo Estate

Barossa Valley
- 46   The Barossa Cellar
- 52   Barossa Valley Estate and Gardens
- 58   Seppeltsfield
- 64   Torbreck

Adelaide Hills
- 70   Penfolds Magill Estate
- 78   Shaw + Smith

Langhorne Creek
- 84   Kimbolton

New South Wales

Hunter Valley
- 90   Brokenwood
- 98   Hungerford Hill
- 104   Running Horse

Orange
- 110   Montoro

Mudgee
- 116   Logan

Western Australia

Margaret River
- 122   Amelia Park
- 128   Leeuwin Estate
- 134   Passel Estate
- 140   Vasse Felix

Victoria

Yarra Valley
- 146   Domaine Chandon
- 154   Levantine Hill
- 160   Medhurst
- 166   Oakridge
- 172   TarraWarra
- 178   Yering Station

Mornington Peninsula
- 184   Jackalope Hotel
- 190   Montalto
- 196   Polperro
- 202   Port Phillip Estate
- 208   Pt Leo Estate
- 214   Ten Minutes by Tractor

Nagambie
- 220   Mitchelton

Bellarine Peninsula
- 226   Leura Park

Tasmania

Piper's River
- 230   Clover Hill

Apslawn
- 236   Devil's Corner

Hobart
- 242   Moorilla at MONA

Australian Capital Territory

Canberra
- 248   Shaw Wines

Queensland

Scenic Rim
- 254   The Overflow Estate 1895

260   Credits
262   Index
267   Acknowledgements
268   About the author

Australian winery architecture and design

Wine tourism in Australia has expanded at a rapid pace as wine regions become destinations in their own rights for an increasingly discerning traveller market.

Growth has been fuelled by the evolution of winery design, from functional working vineyards to award-winning cellar doors, restaurants and hotels, as estates look to satisfy visitors' appetites for unique and exciting physical environments.

Wineries across the globe now regularly engage leading architects to create extraordinary, original constructions that complement the winemaking and tasting experiences.

In Europe, world-renowned studios have rejuvenated winery and cellar-door architecture for some of the biggest names in the wine industry.

Winery designers in Spain include Foster + Partners, Rogers Stirk Harbour, the late Zaha Hadid, Frank Gehry and Santiago Calatrava. Renzo Piano and Mario Botta are active in Italy, while Jean Nouvel, Christian Portzamparc and Phillipe Starck have made their mark in France.

Château La Coste in France famously embodied the blossoming relationship between architecture and wine by commissioning Tadao Ando, Frank Gehry, Jean Nouvel and Renzo Piano to design buildings across the estate.

Australia has fully embraced this progression as domestic wineries scoop architecture awards, in addition to their traditional hauls of wine and restaurant medals.

Often defined as a combination of art and science, winemaking encompasses five stages of development: harvesting, crushing and pressing, fermentation, clarification, ageing and bottling. It is how vintners adopt and combine these distinct elements that make their wine unique.

Architecture similarly embraces art and science through its own five-stage design process: concept design, design development, authority approval, construction documentation, and contract administration.

How the architect responds to a winery brief, budget constraints and the restrictions and opportunities presented by the site during these stages leads to an architectural style as individual as the wine itself.

One wine estate, for example, sought to create an 'Alice in Wonderland' journey that takes the visitor down a proverbial rabbit hole, while another's remit required an environmentally friendly 'treehouse' construction comprised of old shipping containers that blend in with the surrounding vineyards.

Whether there was a need for careful juxtaposition of existing structure and new building, the incorporation of local materials or specific winemaking techniques, all these distinctive wineries have one thing in common – a desire to nurture and embolden the traditional winemaking and tasting experience.

The first impressions when arriving at any winery are formed by the architecture and design of the building and vineyard. While a rustic appearance had charm in the past, nowadays the wine-tasting traveller is more appreciative of memorable structures that supplement the wine tasting itself.

One key factor in this progression is the realisation by wine estates that architects are able to manage financial and timescale goals while bringing their distinct winery vision to fruition.

Among almost 1,000 cellar doors situated across the wine regions in Australia, the 40 projects featured in this book each demonstrate a uniqueness in their approach to their design visions, and serve to inform and illustrate the exciting new direction in Australian winery architecture.

How the wine destination and wine-tasting experience have been enhanced is explored in each chapter, where winemakers, owners, architects and designers provide personal insights, perspectives and individual stories.

Find out what inspired their designs and how they worked together to create and celebrate the collaboration of wine and design.

d'Arenberg Cube
McLaren Vale

Solving the puzzle

The astonishing d'Arenberg Cube presents an unforgettable surrealist addition to a longstanding winery in the McLaren Vale region. The original homestead property was built back in the 1880s.

Inspired by the complexities and puzzles of winemaking, owner and fourth-generation vigneron Chester Osborn formed his idea in 2003 for a truly original cube-shaped building.

"I first approached the architect, Nic Salvati from ADS Architects, with the concept of colours and three-by-three cubes which we canned fairly quickly. Then, eventually, I came up with the idea of four-by-four, with a complex geometric pattern on the outside as the building."

Chester's family have been growing grapes and making wine since 1912, using traditional methods in the winery and vineyard, while Chester himself worked vintages in other wineries before becoming d'Arenberg's chief winemaker in 1984.

Chester presented his idea to the d'Arenberg board back in 2004, recalling: "They thought it was crazy and it would never happen." But of course it did, and he became involved in every facet of the design of the building.

Envisioning an iconic attraction that everyone would want to visit, Chester references the Sydney Opera House as an example of how to stand out in its environment while making full use of a superlative view.

The d'Arenberg Cube was set within the middle of the vineyard so that "it looked like it was plonked in there," while the ground floor cladding is set back with mirrors to give the impression the building is floating in the air.

The intricate and complex building design process proved quite challenging and Chester recalls complications during construction, which were subsequently overcome. "Most of the time I was told it can't be done and then I would go and do some work and draw a picture and then yes it was possible."

The Cube's five levels are specifically designed to entice and excite the senses, resulting in a stimulating wine destination whose features include a wine sensory room, a virtual fermenter, a 360-degree video room and other tactile experiences.

Visitors are encouraged to experience the Alternate Realities Museum, located on the ground floor, which houses numerous art installations, while the Blending Bench provides an opportunity to create individual wines that can be blended, bottled and labelled to take home.

On the top storey, a wine-tasting room offers panoramic views over the wine region, the Willunga Hills and Gulf St Vincent, and an adjacent café includes a casual food offering. In addition, guests can experience behind-the-scenes tours of vintage wines and wine masterclasses.

The journey through the Cube evokes a sense of history of the wine and how it is made, while the Salvador Dalí exhibition adds another twist with an authentic take on the art world.

The resultant five-storey d'Arenberg Cube was deemed sufficiently prestigious to be officially opened by the premier of South Australia in 2016. The building has attracted enormous publicity, with the media using models of the Cube to promote tourism in Australia.

The winery has received countless awards under Chester's watch – for wines, winery, winemaker and restaurant – as its reputation as a distinctive brand has grown regionally, nationally and internationally. Broadening this already extensive roll of honour, numerous prizes have now been garnered in recognition of the design and construction of the architectural project, including a prestigious Good Design Award in 2016.

Chester concedes, "It is unusual in the world for a cellar door to be this elaborate in style," and it has certainly made the McLaren Vale region much more popular.

Feedback from enthralled visitors includes the terms 'amazement', 'Willy Wonka' and 'Mad Hatter'. Customers arrive in the morning and spend the day at the Cube, partaking in the blending class, lunch and art exhibition, with Chester claiming when they leave, "they feel like they have been on another planet."

While many buildings can look interesting on the outside but merely functional and mundane on the inside, the d'Arenberg Cube is even more bizarre on the inside than on the outside, surprising and delighting all who enter.

Chester is known for making 'the loudest wines', a bold claim and adjective that could equally well apply to the fulfilment of his cubic-cellar-door vision as a statement work of art and amazing architecture.

Beresford
McLaren Vale

Less is more

A family-owned South Australian winery purchased in 1985 by industry legend Rob Dundon and wife Bronwyn, Beresford winery dominates an elevated McLaren Vale location, 130 metres (427 feet) above sea level.

From such heights, vines are dry-grown in the ancient sandy soils of a 28-hectare (70-acre) vineyard, creating wines of intense and nuanced flavours that are best sampled while enjoying panoramic views from Beresford House and Beresford Tasting Pavilion.

The concept for the Tasting Pavilion was inspired by the Napa Valley in the United States, where Californians use wine cellars as tasting rooms.

"We felt that there was nothing quite like it in Australia, so we decided to build a modern, contemporary version where we could showcase our Beresford wine brand," the owners note.

It was envisioned that the space would replicate a modern-day, open-plan living style, where the key elements are simplicity of form, design and execution.

Local Adelaide business Alexander Brown Architects, in collaboration with Enoki Design, were engaged to design and deliver the Tasting Pavilion, meeting the client's brief to provide an environment that celebrates Beresford wines.

Based on previous experience with the designers, it was believed that they could interpret the desired style and execute the brief the best. "They [the clients] wanted to create a building that provided a unique and interactive wine-tasting experience, highlighting the beautiful property and sprawling vineyards," director Alexander Brown recalls.

Together, they explored the ideas and juxtaposition of winemaking: the earthiness of the grapes, the vines and the sophistication of the winemaking process through to the wine-tasting experience.

The resulting spaces provide a visionary place to experience the wine, and have been built with precision and attention to detail, in a stunning contemporary and modern style.

South Australia

A minimal aesthetic of clean lines and monochromatic colours creates a beautiful and dramatic backdrop for wine tasting and product display. There is a restrained use of high-quality materials such as solid oak and in-situ poured concrete.

The black timber external cladding is refined and the detailing complements the interior screening, forming a seamless integration between the architecture and interior, aiming to reflect the precise nature of the Beresford brand.

Alexander explains how the sustainably sourced timber cladding was knotted and imperfect, and the exposed screws and polished finish of the concrete floor all enhance "this idea of rawness, however, our execution of the design demonstrates the refinement in these design elements and sophistication of the Beresford brand and philosophy through its sleek exterior and minimal interior."

It is extremely modern for a winery cellar door, yet the use of natural materials and expansive use of glass reduce the impact of the structure on the landscape setting. According to the architect, "this elegance will only grow, with the timber building ensuring a timeless and graceful ageing."

The combination of timber screens and glass provide an interactive and ever-changing façade and play of light within the space. The Tasting Pavilion can be opened up on warm days, naturally cooling the interior, and closed off during the winter months, utilising the heat generated from the suspended fireplace.

There is visibility through the screens that maintains a connection to the vines, and the sliding screens respond to the change in seasons, maintaining an interactive sense of place.

Beresford wanted to create a facility that allows visitors to take in the landscape of the beautiful vines during all seasons. The Tasting Pavilion is popular in the summer months, with a relaxed outside atmosphere, sitting and looking onto the grape-filled vines; and in the cooler months visitors spend time sitting in the tasting room, warmed by the fireplace.

The concept was to involve the 'outside-in' feel, when the sliding timber doors were opened, it was as if you were sitting among nature.

Completed in 2016 by builders BuildInc, the venue now plays host to a variety of corporate and private functions including weddings. It expresses Beresford's vision of a high-end yet highly personal tasting experience, and articulates the philosophy behind the wine brand.

Part of the vision was for the space to be well integrated into the existing environment and host 'concierge-style' wine tasting matched with seasonal local produce.

Beresford considers the pavilion to be 'one of a kind in the region'. It differs with the simplicity of design and interactive nature of the space within the one room. It certainly showcases the estate and its products in a space that is comfortable, luxurious and engaging to all the senses.

Dowie Doole
McLaren Vale

Sustainable vision

Dowie Doole's estate vineyards are located in two of McLaren Vale's most distinct and prized terroirs: the sandy soils of Blewitt Springs and the ancient rocks of Tatachilla, whose geology dates back 650 million years.

Founders Drew Dowie and Norm Doole realised the potential of the estate vineyard in 1995 and formed a partnership to nurture and ensure the sustainability of these living landscapes for future generations.

The visionary pair passed the baton on 20 years later to chief winemaker Chris Thomas, who purchased the winery with several like-minded enthusiasts, while Norm retains a presence as chair and shareholder.

Heralding the new Dowie Doole era, Chris looked to construct a new cellar door that would proudly showcase the best of the Australian lifestyle and Australian wine to the world.

"The vision was for the design to deliver an immersive, intimate and educational experience, while staying true to the beliefs of our founders of sustainability, community and creativity," he says.

The initial design brief presented to the architect was to craft a space that delivered on these visions and beliefs, in part by utilising shipping containers used to transport their wine.

Oli Scholz of Scholz Vinali had been recommended to undertake the design, and during their first meeting on-site, Chris knew Oli was ideal for the job as they walked around the vineyard and began discussing potential sites for the tasting room.

"We were standing near a large area of rubble from deposited dirty fill, when Oli pointed out that a key principle of sustainable architecture, rather than take a clean site and build on it, is to take a previously disturbed site and convert it to something beautiful," remembers Chris.

Oli suggested considering the location full of dirty fill as a strong potential site, which also benefitted from being in a sheltered position immersed within the centre of the vineyard.

"I thought at that moment, Oli really understood the fundamental elements of the project and would be perfect for the project," Chris recalls.

For his part, the architect was aware of the client's love of container architecture and proposed a design that would complement and enhance the brand.

"The choice of materials speaks of the company's push towards sustainable practices … and the vineyard is now certified sustainable," Oli states.

Formed by deftly adapting four shipping containers, shaded by an expressive, sawtooth-esque roofline, Dowie Doole's new cellar door, named the Tasting Pod, sits nestled among 1965 Grenache vine plantings and their prized Shiraz vineyard, Rock Paddock.

The Corten exterior is slowly developing its characteristic rich, rust patina in tone and texture. The built space is expanded by a large timber deck, highlighted by a stone wall built from rocks recovered from the adjacent vineyard, and surrounded by paths laid with Willunga slate.

The interstitial space between the containers creates organising elements, providing activated circulation, breezeways, light pools, places to linger and framing for the landscape views.

Exterior touch points express a considered yet rough and raw material palette, which is then transformed on entering the interior, where the same materials have been refined, polished and oiled to provide a warm, unique and tactile experience for visitors.

Underpinning every detail is a commitment to sustainability, ultimate functionality and flexibility. It is designed to function perfectly for a handful of friends and also open out to facilitate large groups of visitors. One of the critical design principles was for the space to be workable for one person to manage the cellar door during quieter times, and still meet or exceed visitors' expectations.

Oli believes that principles of sustainability, community and creativity are immediately apparent in the building design and the way "it touches the ground lightly". It transforms how people engage with the vineyard landscape, providing a critical identity to the brand and an activated experience of place, he suggests. "The generous decks, the various internal and external pockets as well as the vast lawn invite for casual visits, allowing people to linger and savour Dowie Doole's exquisite wines."

The Dowie Doole cellar door was awarded commendations for both Small Project Architecture and Sustainable Architecture in the AIA South Australia Architecture Awards in 2020.

This new venture has quickly become a popular destination for wine lovers visiting McLaren's wine region, due to its unusual design and immediately recognisable sustainable features.

Chris believes the architecture is a key factor in a winery's drawcard as a destination, just a 40-minute drive from Adelaide.

"Not only is interesting architecture aligned with the art/craft of winemaking, it also adds a layer of interest beyond the wine-tasting experience. Wine is immersive by its nature, so I believe that everything around the tasting experience needs to reflect that," he concludes.

After the success of the initial cellar-door design, Chris and Oli are now in discussion to design an accompanying restaurant and mobile accommodation in little pods that would sit among the vines.

Mitolo
McLaren Vale

Strong and gentle

Mitolo wines has its roots in Abruzzo, southern Italy, where the eponymous family emigrated from in the 1950s and whose regional ethos – *forte e gentile,* meaning strong and gentle – helped turn their market gardening business into an Australian horticultural giant.

Adelaide-born Frank Mitolo initially worked in management within The Mitolo Group – the biggest exporter of potatoes and onions in South Australia and producer of the country's fourth-largest extra virgin olive oil brand – before turning his attention to winemaking.

Starting to make wine as a hobby in 1995 and subsequently completing a grape-growing course, Frank held a five-hour meeting with acclaimed vintner Ben Glaetzer in 1999, which culminated in a six-word, back-of-a-napkin business plan, encompassing individuality, integrity, quality, purity, elegance and power.

The first vintage in 2000, the Mitolo G.A.M. Shiraz, was named after his children, Gemma, Alex and Marco, with the range subsequently expanded to a further 16 wines, each demonstrating its own distinct characteristics.

The winery works closely with its growers, old friends and fellow Italian immigrants, the Lopresti family, who employ Italian varieties and techniques. Business meetings are held over long Sunday lunches where traditional Italian food is shared alongside the Mitolo wine.

Mitolo soon achieved national and international recognition with its sales expanding to more than 20 countries around the world, while securing outstanding reviews and consistently high scores from notable wine critics.

"In my life it's all about family and friends. A table served with food and wine made with passion and love. This is the essence of Mitolo," Frank opines.

A cellar-door tasting room and restaurant development was completed in 2017, marking the next stage in the Mitolo family success story.

The stunning, architecturally designed composition of black shipping containers is set within the picturesque vines of the McLaren Vale wine region, providing a flexible and functional space for the winery.

Frank approached Tectvs Architects in 2015 to investigate the possibility of a 'pop-up' cellar door, on the premise that a growing wine exporter would be simply re-purposing obsolete containers and economically establishing a cellar door where the grapes are grown.

"My wife, Kirsty Marie, and I spent a lot of time with Tectvs making sure that the design gave the right experience to our customers when visiting," Frank recalls. "The combination of containers, concrete and wood has cleverly given a contemporary yet warm feel to the venue, all the while being very respectful of the beautiful surroundings including the vineyards and natural creek. We feel this gives a greater focus to the wine-tasting experiences; to hero the wine without having too many competing visual or aural interference."

"The brief was for a flexible arrangement that could grow incrementally, first off as a modest cellar door with limited food offers. What started as just six shipping containers has now grown to 12 as the offering continues to expand and evolve," remembers architect Francesco Bonato, director at Tectvs.

The overall design concept was based on the idea of an Italian *sagra*, where the structure and function of the containers are united under a floating roof, much like an Italian festival where food and wine are celebrated with family and friends.

Theoretically, the entire building could be dismantled and moved to another site, just like the temporary and transportable nature of town festivals in Italy.

Francesco emphasises how he sought to distinguish the building from standard structures around the region while responding to the site and context.

"The incumbent approach in McLaren Vale was 'loud and proud'. Instead we chose to be minimal and invisible, out of respect for the sensitivity of the natural environment the cellar door was sited in," he recalls. "There was also a genuine desire to break away from the traditional 'colonial' paradigm for winery buildings. This was very much the contrary approach at the time."

Although not creating a new concept in winery cellar-door design, the architects have succeeded in bringing the unconventional nature of the complex into alignment with the wine brand and cultural ancestry of the family owner.

"It was synthesising these paradigms and inverting them into a building for what is a luxury wine brand and now equally luxurious restaurant and wedding venue," says Francesco.

Frank is understandably appreciative of a building that was awarded The Keith Neighbour Award for Commercial Architecture by the SA chapter of the Australian Institute of Architects in 2019.

"The client continues to embrace the ethos of the building, continuing to expand the facility using the paradigm of shipping containers while respecting the substance of the original architecture," according to Francesco.

Frank surmises the point of difference for this wine destination: "We feel that it is the surprise of discovering the venue when you arrive. Its striking yet sympathetic placement among its surroundings."

"As you walk inside it's really more than you expect: contemporary, compact, practical and only housing what is necessary. We are not positioned on the highest mountain, but rather surrounded by understated landscape views of vines, the natural creek and the Willunga Hills."

Primo Estate
McLaren Vale

Maintaining Italian roots

The story of Primo Estate begins in the Le Marche region of Italy, the birthplace of founder Primo Grilli, who emigrated to Australia in 1953 to study winemaking and realise his dream of creating a modern vineyard reflective of his Italian roots.

Established in 1973, Primo Estate's home vineyard, located in South Australia's McLaren Vale wine region, was passed on six years later to sons Peter and Joe, who graduated as Dux of Winemaking from Roseworthy Agricultural College.

Joe helped secure the estate's unique reputation, combining up-to-date Australian know-how with old-school Italian winemaking heritage, as he put into practice the radical techniques learnt.

Following a reflective, decade-long planning period, Joe and wife, Dina, opened their stunning new headquarters in 2006, incorporating a cellar door and tasting room, which combined new-world influences with classic Italian practicality, underscoring the multicultural influence of the wines.

In addition to a formal seated and casual bar wine-tasting venue, the building's remit envisioned a courtyard with outdoor seating and a wood oven to form an Australian interpretation of a small Italian square – a *piazzetta*, timeless in its design approach.

"We wanted to create a distinctive, authentic experience that could only take place in one very special spot in the entire world. The architecture plays a strong part in communicating the Primo Estate vision: Italian-inspired design in the heart of McLaren Vale," said general manager and third-generation vintner, Matteo Grilli.

Matteo stressed the importance of developing a building with a human scale, noting that though such a vast winery could comfortably accommodate a far larger cellar door, the emphasis was on offering the same intimacy and proportion experienced when walking into any public square in Italy.

Joe and Dina returned from their extensive Italian travels with hundreds of photos and stories of beautiful squares and hillside towns to share with the designer. Their brief was clear – a contemporary cellar door based on the traditional square that captures the conviviality of an Italian town.

Michael Harvey and Bruce Watson of Edwards Design, alongside interior designer and estate family member Lisa Zamberlan, were able to draw on an intimate knowledge of the winery brand and vision – a prime reason behind the project's success, according to Matteo.

Michael Harvey concurred, noting: "I think every winemaker, winery and cellar door does things differently, so this project was really about us understanding how the business worked and how they wanted it to work in the future."

The building, interiors and landscape were designed by Edwards Design, with local partner Chapman Herbert Architects providing documentation and contract administration services.

Edwards Design started with the idea of the square concept and developed the required spaces around it, incorporating each of the four surrounding walls as sculptural elements, arranged in an asymmetrical composition reminiscent of a hillside town built up over the centuries. The courtyard's centrepiece is a wall constructed from locally sourced stone that houses the pizza oven specially imported from Italy.

An enclosed sun-trapped area providing protection from the wind, the courtyard – which Matteo identifies as his favourite part of the winery – operates as an in-demand outdoor dining and function space, where the pizza oven and outdoor wood-fired grill deliver a nostalgic backdrop for Italian feasts.

The venue hosts an established calendar of events, from car launches to regional food demonstrations, that revolve around the architecture and design. The careful placement of deciduous trees contributes to the amenity of the space, creating distinctly different scenes throughout the year as the seasons change.

The architecture provides a platform for presenting the wines with floor-to-ceiling windows, offering sweeping views of the vineyards and visibility from any point in the internal courtyard. The wine-tasting experience is enhanced by this ability to point out to the regional vineyards where the wine comes from.

Inside there are references to the wine label through colour and design, resulting in a tranquil setting that allows people to relax and focus on the simple act of tasting the wine. Further nods to the owners' origins are found among Italian features, from the ceiling wallpaper to the Venetian glass chandeliers in the VIP room.

Deliberately hidden from the road, the building is accessed via a winding drive through the vineyard. From the car park, visitors walk on between two groves of olive trees before arriving in the sheltered courtyard.

Because the site is private, the architectural expression was free from any contextual constraints, and rural references were deliberately shunned.

According to Michael, the design is essentially a sculpture in the landscape; four volumes of four materials, arranged around the central core, creating an abstract ensemble among the vines.

Interestingly, Matteo recalls that when the building was completed, guests would remark on how radical and progressive the design was for the region. Its distinctive modernity caused quite a stir in a neighbourhood that largely comprised metal sheds and older buildings.

Guests subsequently commented on how calm and connected it is to the landscape – almost the exact opposite of initial reactions – with its individuality now derived from core design principles, combining the Italian *piazzetta* with the modernity of contemporary winemaking.

The Barossa Cellar
Barossa Valley

Museum of wine

The Barossa Cellar is a state-of-the-art wine museum created by Barons of Barossa (a group founded by influential Barossa wine industry members) to house the largest collection of premium wines produced in the Barossa and Eden Valley regions.

The first museum of its kind in Australia has three main roles: to provide a regional centre for the promotion of the local wine community, to educate a global audience about Barossa wine, and to cellar a magnificent collection of fine wines generously donated by Barossa wineries.

This extraordinary community project was made possible through the support of local wineries, growers, families and businesses, as well as wine enthusiasts from around the world.

Because it does not sell wine, The Barossa Cellar is not a cellar door. It instead operates by collecting and preserving the best wines from each vintage and cellars for them for a minimum of 10 years.

The Barossa Cellar is a repository and showcase for promoting Barossa wine locally and globally, by hosting masterclasses, tastings, seminars and other wine education and promotion experiences.

It is owned and operated by Barons of Barossa on behalf of the Barossa community. The not-for-profit organisation was founded in 1975 to support local wine, viticulture, gastronomy, arts and heritage.

The Barons purchased the 3-hectare (7.5-acre) greenfield site between the townships of Tanunda and Angaston in 2016, and built into the side of a hill to leave the cellar section effectively underground while its offices overlook the valley.

The Barossa Grape and Wine Association (BGWA) signed an agreement to become the sole tenant for 20-plus years, demonstrating the venture's long-term vision.

The vineyard, newly planted in 2020, aims to reflect best-practice viticulture and showcase what local grape growers have learnt over 175 years. Key stakeholders and those who have donated vines as part of fundraising activities will be given first option to purchase the limited-release wines produced here.

The impressive structure was designed by Barossa-based architecture firm JBG Architects, who had previously worked with St Hugo, Hentley Farm, Grant Burge Wines, Shaw + Smith, Yalumba, Henschke, Angove Family Winemakers and others.

Jamie Gladigau, owner of JBG, was excited to bring together all that experience into one building. The architect's involvement began in 2013 when he set about defining what The Barossa Cellar should look like. "We were incredibly honoured, and armed with a fairly open brief."

"There were plenty of opinions; some expected a grand statement, some expected a beacon for exclusive wine, a museum of culture, food, books," Jamie remembers. But at the time there was no site, and as winemakers take their inspiration from the vineyard, "architects certainly take their inspiration from the site." Images were presented to a marquee full of Barons to kick-start interest, so without a site the first concept sketches were theoretical. "An underground space for a Barossa long lunch, prepared by our local chefs and surrounded by hundreds of open boxes of wine. The building must be buried into the side of a hill, I thought, and capture an indelible valley view. The whole experience, to leave you wanting to come again … for more."

Jamie explains how this last comment ultimately shaped the architectural design. "I believe the essence of what our Barossa community offers visitors is one of humble service. We know our finest is as good as anywhere in the world so we don't need to put it all on the table in the first minute. We can layer experiences and leave visitors to find their own place."

Development of these ideas continued for six years, and ultimately the brief was to create a place that was contemporary and sustainable, and that represented the Barossa's heart and soul. It also needed to safely store 100,000 wines.

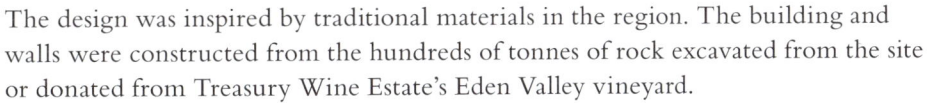

The design was inspired by traditional materials in the region. The building and walls were constructed from the hundreds of tonnes of rock excavated from the site or donated from Treasury Wine Estate's Eden Valley vineyard.

Jamie ensured the orientation of the building maximised the views and sunlight, and based his design approach on using conventional materials in innovative ways.

The 30-metre-long (99-foot-long) wine vault showcases wines in specially designed displays, while a magnificent curved ceiling is constructed of black-steel gabion cages containing exposed natural stones above.

The grand hall, running through the centre of the building, can seat 100 guests or be divided into three separate spaces for smaller industry workshops, meetings or tastings.

Chairman of The Barossa Cellar, Louisa Rose, notes, "The Barossa Cellar's design not only meets the practical requirements for cellaring fine wines, but has created an inspiring, multi-purpose, open space in the grand hall, suitable for sit-down dinners for 100, small meetings, seminars and wine tastings."

"We are thrilled with the response from visitors to The Barossa Cellar who recognise it as a subtle, yet significant landmark. They particularly love how The Barossa Cellar is nestled between a stunning vineyard in the foreground and a spectacular backdrop of gums," she adds.

Jamie concludes, "What we've got is a simple, honest building, buried into the hillside, with layered experiences, brought to life by the enormous generosity of all involved … contributing to the authenticity of Brand Barossa."

Barossa Valley

Barossa Valley Estate and Gardens
Barossa Valley

A sophisticated blend

Exquisitely positioned in the heart of the Barossa Valley in the historic township of Marananga, Barossa Valley Estate overlooks one of the foremost red-wine regions in the world.

A relative newcomer to the area, Barossa Valley Estate has been proud to celebrate and expand the region's formidable red-wine heritage by producing only high-quality Shiraz, Cabernet Sauvignon and Grenache Shiraz Mourvèdre.

The unique warm climate and red clay soils that create these varietals underscore the Estate's philosophy to "capture the distinctive elegance, finesse and vibrant flavours of the Barossa Valley".

Established in 1985, the Estate was forged from a group of growers who banded together to convert great grapes into great wines.

In 2013, new owners Delegat Group Limited of New Zealand renovated the existing facilities and grounds in line with their vision to create an unforgettable experience for visiting wine lovers.

DesignInc, an architectural practice with studios throughout Australia, were engaged to undertake the works, further to the original facility design by director Richard Stafford in 1999.

"It was very rewarding to revisit and refresh a building that was an important project early in my career. The wine industry has evolved significantly since the building was originally designed and consumer expectations are higher," notes Richard. "The new facility offers a bespoke experience that reflects the brand vision to connect the wine to a sense of place within the Barossa."

The brief called for a revitalisation of the interiors and stronger connections with their surrounds. With vines growing right up the to the cellar door, visitors can now experience the region's great wines while overlooking the vineyards that created them. The structure was retained, and the stone spine wall and pavilion-style roof remain, as do the framed views of the ranges and village.

In response to the opportunities presented, the aim was for the architecture and landscape, and wine and landscape to be interwoven.

Jim Delegat and DesignInc worked with internationally renowned landscape designer Paul Bangay to create a setting that embodies and enhances the Barossa Valley Estate wines and brand experience, famously emboldened by the largest perennial gardens in Australia.

A suite of decks, terraces and arbours connect and integrate the building into its environs. Collaboration with Paul on the hard landscaping, finishes and detailing ensured alignment and consistency.

Visitors are invited to explore the beautiful Estate gardens where all seasons are celebrated, much like the seasonality of the wines.

Stunning outdoor areas have been designed to offer settings for small and large groups to gather, taste the wine and take in the views, and stone walls throughout have been constructed from the region's local excavated stones, reflecting the historical nature of the site.

Describing the design experience, Richard says: "It begins at the curving driveway that meanders through the landscape, revealing and framing different views, which create a sense of journey and arrival. An imposing stone wall at the end of the car park mimics the spine wall and passing through a small opening in this wall reveals a view of the cellar door and landscape."

A welcoming entrance invites the visitor to step inside the tasting room – a light and airy space where the open-plan layout allows views from every position. The tasting counter is located in front of the original stone wall, and there are also stand-alone tasting tables throughout the room for groups or couples to gather for a more intimate experience. The E&E Tasting Room is an additional private setting dedicated to the iconic E&E Black Pepper Shiraz. Traditional Barossa materials are used in a contemporary manner; American oak, limestone and concrete complement the original palette.

"This careful attention to detail that flows between the built form and the landscape embeds the building with a strong sense of place," notes Richard who suggests the cellar door can best be described as "a sophisticated blend of architecture, landscape and wine".

There is a strong and seamless connection between the architecture and landscape, wine and landscape, wine and the Barossa that captures the Barossa Valley Estate experience. "The resulting sum of parts come together to create a unified experience and provide an authentic sense of place within the Barossa Valley," Richard believes.

The combination of the extensive gardens, the contemporary architecture and the stunning location in the heart of the valley makes the Barossa Valley Estate unique and memorable.

Barossa Valley

Seppeltsfield
Barossa Valley

Blending old and new

One of Australia's oldest wineries, Seppeltsfield was established in 1851 by namesake founder Joseph Ernst Seppelt, a German-born viticulturist and merchant, who had immigrated to South Australia with his wife, Johanna, and their three children, two years earlier.

Famous for being the world's only winery to release a 100-year-old, single-vintage wine each year, its recent accolades include being awarded 2017 Global Best of Wine Tourism by the Great Wine Capitals Global Network and winner of the 'Wineries, distilleries or breweries' category in the Qantas Australian Tourism Awards.

The Seppeltsfield estate combines more than 170 hectares (420 acres) of venerable vineyard, gardens and heritage-listed architecture, surrounded by a small settlement in one of the most westerly townships of the picturesque Barossa Valley region.

An avenue of more than 2,000 Canary Island date palm trees line the avenue approaching estate, setting the scene for the grandeur that awaits the visitor.

There are 13 state heritage–listed buildings on the property, and the use of local bluestone and ornate details add to the historical elegance prevalent throughout. A large courtyard with a water feature marks the grand entrance to the tasting room beyond.

A world-class cellar door and tasting rooms, fine-dining restaurant, and contemporary art and design studios create a vibrant community of wine, food and art, continuing the 'village' vision of the Seppelt family to welcome travellers.

The Seppelts had originally intended to farm tobacco, but later generations focused on grape growing and winemaking as they helped shape the Australian wine-industry story. The family is regarded as one of the country's most successful wine dynasties, who maintained ownership of the estate from 1850 to 1985.

In 2007, the estate returned to private ownership and Warren Randall, a viticulturist and winemaker who worked for the family in the 1980s, purchased 50 percent in 2009. He had plans to redevelop the winery including all of its tourism assets, and in 2012 a tourism master plan was created, including the remodelling of the original Bottling Hall.

Barossa Valley

Blending historical and contemporary architecture, destination restaurant FINO and the cellar door are located in the redeveloped 1900 building, where circular tasting alcoves create unique and intimate settings for the wine-tasting experience.

These innovative pods were installed to manage the large number of visitors and allow a maximum ratio of tasting space for guests. As well as functional and convenient, they are viewed as sculptural objects in the large vibrant space.

The design vision according to Seppeltsfield was to "create a modern feel with cues to the history and heritage of the building". Max Pritchard Architect was engaged to undertake the major revitalisation works, in light of their international recognition for designing tourism projects, personal attention and as a South Australian local business.

The brief emphasised cellar-door tourism and provision for a restaurant. Director Max Pritchard recalls, "We explored possibilities of designing a new cellar door as an iconic structure but the old bottling hall from the 1880s was such a wonderful space with its exposed stone and high lantern, trussed roof." The new work focused on restoring the space to its original impressive character.

A mezzanine was inserted to facilitate access to the world-famous 150-year-old fortified-wine collection, inspired by a recently discovered unbuilt sketch drawing by the original architect. New steps were formed down to the old concrete and brick wine vats, where the walls and lids were removed to create a unique dining space. A restrained colour and material palette was deliberately selected, which comprises recycled slate, oak reflecting the wine-barrel tradition, and industrial black and white.

A challenge for the design team was the location of the hall, partly underground, which made it difficult to create an open, welcoming entry. Considerable excavation formed the sunken courtyard and landscaping helped achieve the desired reinforcement of the site's history. "The architectural aim was to highlight the beauty of the existing structures but adapt for the new use," Max notes. The architect, client and builder worked closely together to ensure this outcome, without compromising the original building fabric.

Max believes the architecture emphasises the role of tradition in winemaking through its careful adaption of the heritage buildings, which can be appreciated by guided tours of the multi-year winner of *Gourmet Traveller WINE* magazine's Star Cellar Door of the Barossa Valley.

Torbreck
Barossa Valley

International Following

Torbreck blends a gentle Mediterranean climate with a Silesian and English grape-growing heritage and European winemaking style, dating back to the 1840s when the first vines were planted in the Barossa Valley.

Multi-generational growers underpin the Torbreck journey, which has inspired investments in some of the most precious vineyards across the valley and the construction of a winery and bottling line in 2008 that ensures total quality control of its produce. The subsequent expansion of the original settler's cottage cellar door in 2017 sought to establish an international guest centre where friends and collectors from Australia and overseas would feel part of Torbeck's quest to create its finest wines yet.

"The vision was to develop a visitor centre where we could host and entertain our tourism visitors and international buyers and guests and give them a true Barossa experience," says Michael Van Der Sommen, direct sales and brand manager at Torbreck. "We wanted the cellar door to reflect the Torbreck brand – timeless, quality focussed, handmade and Barossan, while remaining personal and intimate."

Barossa-based JBG Architects were commissioned in 2014 to develop a boutique cellar door in line with new ownership strategies to promote Torbreck wines to high-end connoisseurs around the world.

Jamie Gladigau, project director and principal of JBG Architects, remembers their response to the brief was to carefully curate an addition of modern architecture to the 150-year-old cottage. "Our intention was to contrast strong forms, each highlighting the other, while tied by consistent materials and a simple colour palette. While the cottage is heavily grounded, the rear pavilion floats above the sloping site, displaying Torbreck winery and vineyard estate via an external arbour. The result is our interpretation of an international design style utilising indigenous materials and construction techniques, contrasting sympathetically with the existing historic cottage which has housed German settlers, young renters and, more recently, Torbreck's quaint wine sales outlet."

A light-filled glass pavilion accommodates both the private and structured wine-tasting spaces and allows the flow of guests to be managed within the different areas for different experiences.

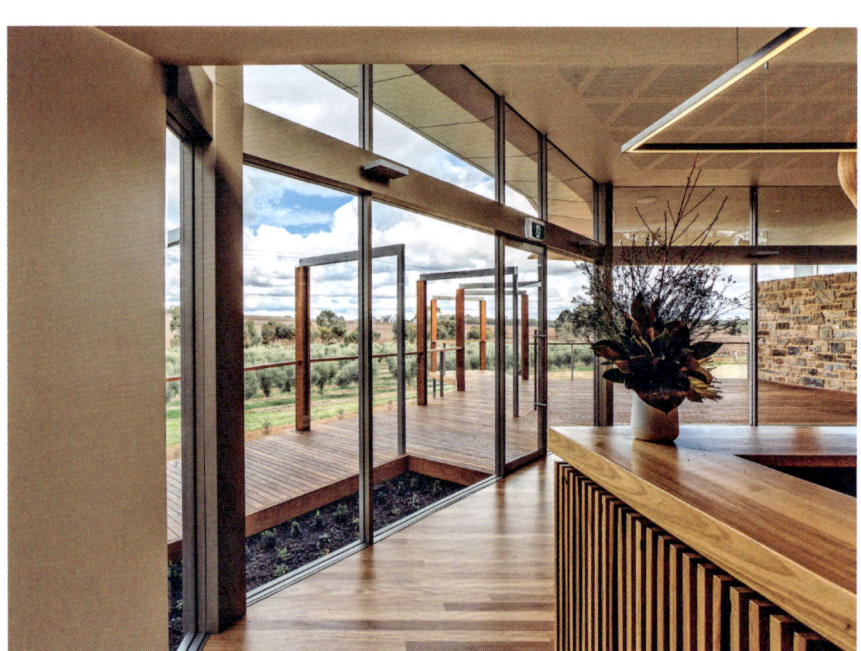

At its heart sits the temperature-controlled wine room that has become Michael's favourite part of the winery. The space showcases one bottle of every vintage of every wine that Torbreck has produced, and in every size across the entire range, from 750-millilitre to 6-litre Imperial to the 12-litre Balthazar.

Floating above the landscape, the 150-square-metre (1,615-square-foot) addition responds to the slope of the site and frames the views of the adjoining vineyard. Its orientation maximises natural light, and the design intent throughout embraces the preservation of its heritage setting. Touchpoints are provided to enhance the brand, and the materials palette references the methods of winemaking in its simplicity and sophistication. Stone has been sourced locally, timber reused from old wine barrels, and the use of local builders and artisans has resulted in an understated sense of quality and craftsmanship.

Although there were challenges when designing and constructing the extension building while retaining the fabric and integrity of the 1880s cottage, Torbreck is pleased that the old workmanship charm was preserved and blends naturally into the new building.

Visitors see the merging of the old and new of the Barossa through the built form, see this reflected in the brand ethos, before enjoying the wine-tasting event.

For this globally recognised label, the focus is on exceptionally high standards across the vineyards, winemaking and packaging, and Torbreck views its cellar door as an ultra-premium international wine destination.

Guests are often familiar with the brand before they arrive, so Torbreck works hard to ensure the wine experience meets these heightened expectations, while the expansion in visitor numbers has, in turn, exceeded the owners' hopes.

Barossa Valley

Penfolds Magill Estate
Adelaide Hills

Home of Grange

Driven by the merging of science, art and innovation through generations of visionaries and innovators, Penfolds has secured an enviable reputation as one of Australia's most respected winemakers and iconic international brands.

Penfolds Magill Estate, the spiritual birthplace of Australia's most famous winemaking, was established in 1844, when founders Christopher and Mary Rawson Penfold arrived from England and planted vine cuttings carried on their voyage.

Mary ran the rapidly expanding winery, which was producing one-third of all South Australian wine by the time she handed the reins over to daughter Georgina in 1884.

Max Schubert became Penfold's first chief winemaker in 1948 and ran with the innovative tradition as he declared: "All winemakers should possess a good fertile imagination if they are to be successful in their craft."

Max put Penfolds on the global map with his initially secret experimentation of long-lasting wines, which led to the creation of Penfolds Grange in the 1950s.

In 1959, the tradition of 'bin wines' began when the first wine, a Shiraz grown in the company's own Barossa Valley vineyards, was named after the storage area of the cellars where it is aged. Thus Kalimna Bin 28 became the first official Penfolds bin number wine.

Penfolds Grange won scores of awards as it evolved into one of the world's most celebrated wine labels, even receiving a heritage listing in South Australia on the 50th anniversary of its birth.

The story of design and mastery is revealed at Magill Estate, which in 2014 set about creating a new centralised cellar-door experience, encompassing tasting rooms; a café; meeting, educational and function spaces; winery tours; and cellars within historic tunnels.

Denton Corker Marshall were appointed architects for the redevelopment, further to their work on many iconic Australian structures including Melbourne Museum, the Australian War Memorial and the Australian Embassy in Tokyo. Their collaboration with one of Australia's most acclaimed wines seems a natural fit.

The resulting design complements the heritage setting and allows visitors to experience the winery's historical roots, including the earliest cellars and their original stone walls. Modern insertions include blackened metal art screens displaying Penfolds wine bottles with their distinctive red caps, and a backlit 'bin wall' which serves as a contemporary interpretation of how the original winemakers aged their wines in bins.

Australian timbers have been combined with traditional winemaking timbers of French and American oak, while the cellar-door bars and joinery are made from Victorian ash timber – burnt by hand to reveal the blackened timber-grain texture of the wood. Such details are simultaneously strong, subtle and stunning, much like the wines the estate produces.

The cellar door and Magill Estate kitchen blend in with the existing buildings, while the kitchen has been positioned in a transparent glass cube, wrapped in metal solar blades. This results in a framing of the heritage heart of the site by two modern bookends, which in turn creates a focus point for visitor sight lines.

The café uses a combination of lighting through the perforated timber, recreating the feeling of dappled sunlight shining through the vines. When dining indoors or on the grand verandah, guests can enjoy the exceptional views over the estate and the nearby city of Adelaide, whose close proximity marks Penfolds as a rare urban vineyard.

"Visitor experience is a core feature of the project, with emphasis on repeat visitation. The relocated cellar door to the front of the precinct within the vineyards is the gateway for all experiences to emanate from, reinforcing its importance and capitalising on sales and marketing opportunities," says Denton Corker Marshall.

Resolution of the cellar door with its fluctuating visitor population required careful design and planning to provide an intimate experience for individuals during quiet times while catering for large weekend crowds. Multiple bespoke tasting rooms, such as the Bin room, and Yattarna and Grange rooms, housed within the oldest cellars on the site, provide unique design and visitor experiences that encourage guests to return.

Interiors by Denton Corker Marshall are described by Penfolds as "artfully blended together with textures, colours and materials inspired by winemaking tools and traditions as well as their vineyards." Furniture was selected in association with designer Pascale Gomes-McNabb.

Historical artefacts uncovered during architectural investigations in the early design phase enabled elements, such as the cupboard where Max Schubert stored the very valuable hidden Grange vintages, to be highlighted in the final design.

A complete collection of Grange magnums dating from the 1970s is honoured in a 'floating' precious box, deep underground – a fitting and satisfying culmination to the winery tour.

In addition to the deliberate nod to the past, there is a focus on the future, both in the winemaking and architecture. At one of Australia's oldest wineries, the years of history, craftsmanship and innovation can be experienced at each touchpoint.

"The redevelopment and enhancements have been designed to expand and improve the visitor experience and education, while preserving the charm, heritage and spirit of the site," according to Penfolds.

The grand entrance off Penfold Road features a front stone wall reminiscent of the past and landscaping along the stately driveway to highlight elements such as the historic Grange Cottage. Magill Estate ably and confidently represents the ultimate showcase of Penfolds heritage, culture and wines.

Shaw + Smith
Adelaide Hills

High-altitude vernacular

Teaming up in 1989, cousins Martin Shaw and Michael Hill Smith co-founded Shaw + Smith and began producing quality wines that best suit the cooler climate of Adelaide Hills, specifically Sauvignon Blanc, Riesling, Chardonnay, Pinot Noir and Shiraz.

Early vintages were made at Wirra Wirra and Petaluma before a further property was purchased at Balhannah to plant more vines and build a winery and tasting room in time for the 2000 vintage.

Shaw + Smith wines are known to be vibrant, exciting and refined while being reflective of their habitat – descriptions that apply equally well to the winery, administration space and tasting-room architecture created by local practice JBG Architects and Melbourne-based Chris Connell Design.

Just as the wetter and colder conditions at high altitude have a significant influence on the production of wine, the building design was shaped by the contextual requirement to withstand the challenging elements.

The owners and joint managing directors requested a smart, well-designed, cost-effective and timeless building that could be easily expanded, while the priority for administration and public spaces was to be simple, functional and stylish. Their vision was inspired by Wynns Winery in Coonawarra, which employs a series of pitched roof forms that can be added to without compromising the original design intent.

JBG Architects were approached just before the turn of the millennium to design the winery building, with Chris Connell engaged to design the interior administration and public spaces.

The architects proposed a series of interconnecting modular units, providing a practical and cost-effective solution for a wine label that could continue to grow. Each unit is 10 metres (33 feet) wide with an insulted double skin of corrugated-metal cladding to the external roof and zinc panelling to the internal ceiling.

Jamie Gladigau of JBG Architects notes that "from a distance, the seven grey gable roof forms resemble a minimal artwork or row of houses."

The original design brief stipulated spaces to be simple, functional and stylish, providing an attractive destination for visitors to the winery. The finishes throughout are modern but timeless, and although the building is now more than 20 years old, it does not look or feel dated.

Martin Shaw believes that the architecture has enhanced the wine-tasting experience by maximising the view, which is his favourite part of the winery. The outlook is a great asset, according to Martin, and the tasting-room design works with the desired sight lines.

The northern aspect is faced with glass to take in the vineyards and distant mountains, while an oversized steel pergola serves as an outdoor space for entertaining. The shadow lines formed by the deck roofing create another visually appealing dimension to the architectural design. "Shaw + Smith are proud of the winery building, a pragmatic but smart and expandable design. Our visitors often comment on what an inviting space we have created to taste and enjoy our wine in," Martin says.

Martin is particularly proud of the building in terms of costs and pragmatism, noting that the architecture "gives what is effectively a tin shed, a smart, timeless look." If given the chance to do anything differently, he admits it would have been nice for the visitor experience to be more interactive with the winemaking activity in the cellar; however, he explains the practical nature of the operation was restrictive in terms of safety and risk of injury.

Overall, both the winery and designers have created a beautiful destination that has stood the test of time and the elements. The winery and cellar door gave new life and refinement to the classic corrugated shed with a unique take on the Australian vernacular.

Kimbolton
Langhorne Creek

Recycling to new heights

More than a century after founder Frank Potts II purchased the original Kimbolton Vineyard in 1911, direct descendants and fifth-generation vigneron siblings Nicole Clark and Brad Case opened their first cellar door, in response to rising customer demand.

"Our existing wine brand was growing rapidly and we needed a home for people to visit to taste and buy our wine in a unique and inviting space," Nicole explains.

The resultant 2018 construct was worth the wait as it promptly scooped the coveted Architecture & Landscape award at the Great Wine Capitals Best of Wine Tourism Awards in 2020, for the innovative design of the cellar door built out of repurposed shipping containers.

The building, located 55 minutes outside Adelaide, combines a unique mix of high-gloss navy industrial shipping containers with recycled timber and feature ply to create an earthy, modern setting among the vines.

It also, literally, elevates wine tasting to greater heights, with an upstairs viewing platform that allows guests to appreciate the beautiful setting among the gum trees and sprawling family-owned vineyards, across the picturesque Langhorne Creek region.

The historic winery chose project architect and builder Damien Chwalisz for his expertise at designing and building with shipping containers and recycled materials. "I had looked at a project Damien had built in Adelaide using shipping containers, contacted him for a meeting and the rest is history," Nicole says. She had been inspired by other winery projects in Australia and overseas that use pre-build methods, and envisioned the containers providing a cost- and time-effective construction build, while demonstrating an authentic architecture that reflects Kimbolton's values.

Damien successfully managed the client's expectations to deliver "architecture that is respectful and acts as backdrop to Kimbolton's beautiful wine."

A surprising amount of work is required to make shipping containers habitable, a task Damien undertook to create a space that is both welcoming and warm internally, while maintaining a robust envelope to the external elements.

Historically, winery or rural businesses lend themselves to a naturally weathering industrial or rustic aesthetic, and in a way Kimbolton respects this tradition through its design intent by creating an almost severe, clean and crisp exterior. Internally, by contrast, the recycled and repurposed timbers, which cover all floors and walls, create a softer and sumptuous space, with the smells of the timber and oils mixing with the tasting notes of the wine.

Kimbolton's aim was to create a cellar door that complemented its surroundings. "There are a lot of natural elements that have been used throughout the project. It was extremely important for us to keep an ambience of as much of the natural landscape as possible, as made very clear by the eucalyptus tree that sprouts through the deck boards straight out from the tasting room," Nicole notes.

When she and Brad set out to build their first cellar door, they never anticipated the widespread and encouraging response they have received from visitors. The importance of the architecture for the winery is reflected by the inclusion of a picture gallery of the structure's construction on Kimbolton's website. "Wines that are conceived in the vineyard, captured in the bottle and speak loudly from the glass," according to the Kimbolton website – adjectives that could equally apply to the architecture.

The cellar door sits elegantly within the geometry of the trees, housed among the reused containers, to send a message of the wine story through its beautifully built form.

"Wineries should act as a destination because people are investing their own time to visit these regions where the architecture and wine are consumed together," Damien states.

Nicole expresses pride in the meticulously paired wine and cheese flights on offer, where four local artisan cheeses are carefully selected to match four Kimbolton wines, a passion project she has presented to customers for many years.

She believes the stunning new building enhances this experience for visitors to the region, because though the use of modular buildings is not a new concept, it does help identify the cellar door's point of difference. "The architecture ties in with our wine marketing and the colour of the shipping containers is what we call Kimbolton Blue as we also use this with our wine labels and on our website. The uniqueness of the shipping containers with the spotted gum slats makes the cellar door look like it was always supposed to be here."

Langhorne Creek

Brokenwood
Hunter Valley

Perfect delivery

One of Australia's best-known and appreciated wine labels has come a long way since the original winery was founded in 1970 by three Sydney-based solicitors and hobby vintners: Tony Albert, John Beeston and James Halliday.

Situated at the foothills of the Brokenback Ranges, 2½ hours from Sydney, the original block was destined to become a community cricket ground before being planted with Cabernet Sauvignon and Shiraz. The first white grapes followed a decade later.

What started out as a boutique, weekend labour of love among friends and families evolved into one of Australia's most reputable wine labels, with the inclusion of six new partners in 1978 leading to the purchase of Graveyard Vineyard next door.

The resultant Graveyard Vineyard Shiraz remains Brokenwood's flagship wine with Langton's Classification of Australian wine listing it as 'exceptional' and the highest ranked red in the Hunter Valley.

Other favourites from the consistently five star–rated winery include the highly acclaimed ILR Reserve Semillon, and the popular Cricket Pitch Range.

The existing cellar door had been in operation since 1983 and undergone two extensions before discussions began in 2014 to create something new.

Space on-site was limited, and to meet the usual local authority requirements, only a long and narrow building form would work. As there was no vineyard to look onto directly, the brief also required the new building to incorporate the existing winery facility.

Managing director and chief winemaker Iain Riggs recalls the original design vision was to offer a total immersion facility with state-of-the-art spaces. The prominent site and architecture should serve to enhance the wine-tasting experience by creating somewhere welcoming, comfortable and aesthetically pleasing.

"It was time to make a proper statement. The new cellar door is the first modern building in many years and enhances the whole of the region. Everyone benefits," Iain says.

Brokenwood whittled down candidates via a competition pitch before appointing Villa + Villa architects to help define the concept and realise their ambitious vision.

Eduardo Villa recalls one of the original requirements was to quintuple annual visitors from 80,000 to 400,000 over a four-year period. He believes the point of difference in winning the competition was their design intent to take customers on a real wine experience, rather than just stand by a bench and sip good wines. Villa + Villa proposed and delivered an overall design that encompassed the building and business model together. The creation of spaces allowing difference experiences encourages the visitor to stay longer and, potentially, spend more money.

"For us, it is extremely important to have a beautiful and successful building that serves the purpose but as the business grows, the building gets the opportunity to shine over and over. The ultimate experience, a shared community, job creation plus a great wine will always deliver an outstanding outcome for our clients," Eduardo notes.

He says the very restrictive nature of the site dictated the specific building placement, which would run parallel to the production complex, and drove the idea to connect both the old and new buildings.

Although this fixed geometry was imposed on the new building, the architects intended for the forms to flow into the landscape and used timber materials on the façade to integrate and assimilate to the surrounding environment.

The purpose-built cellar door features a bold and earthy mix of materials throughout, such as Corten steel, stone, timber, glass and rustic timber palettes used as screens and balustrades.

Covering 1,400 square metres (15,000 square feet), Brokenwood became the largest complex in the Hunter Valley, Australia's most visited wine region, incorporating two dining venues; casual eatery, Cru Bar + Pantry and, more formally, The Wood Restaurant.

Unique features include circular tasting pods, an expansive outdoor terrace with views over the Hunter Valley, private tasting and a wine museum overlooking the working barrel hall. The innovative pods can cater for 20 visitors at a time, far more than standard wine-tasting benches at other cellar doors, which can be limited to four to six patrons.

Brokenwood now provides the options of guided varietal and single-vineyard tastings either around the pods or in the private tasting rooms, behind the scenes tours on aspects of winemaking and winery history, as well as personalised soil-to-cellar experiences.

There is a warm sense of arrival, and the materials are intended to weather over time and age gracefully, much like Brokenwood's wine itself.

Hungerford Hill
Hunter Valley

Regional icon

Hungerford Hill has undergone many changes since Sydney entrepreneur John Parker planted the first vines in 1967, five years before building Australia's first wine tourism complex to incorporate a restaurant.

Sam Amaout took over the reins in 2016, but it was predecessor James Kirby who completed the eye-catching wine complex, then known as One Broke Road and subsequently recognised as an icon of the Hunter Valley.

Kirby, who purchased the winery and cellar door in 2003, lauded the original 'visionary' architect, Walter Barda, who had been approached by previous owner Timothy Tighe in the late 1990s to help formulate a new wine brand and new winery.

"I was asked to prepare a concept plan for the project and ultimately document and oversee the construction phase of the project," Walter recalls. "The site for the project was located at a geographical entry point into the lower Hunter wine region, affording opportunities to create a 'gateway' building, marking a celebratory tone of arrival into Hunter wine country," he says.

The flagship development is situated at the entrance to the Pokolbin district, marking the start of a road that leads into the valley and Upper Hunter. The bold and sculptural forms of Hungerford Hill aptly celebrate the arrival into wine country as visitors are immediately struck by the stunning mountain backdrop and its exquisite positioning within ordered vines. The rooflines respond to the shape of the distant mountains and, in a sense, appear to grow out from the ground.

"With a dramatic backdrop of the Brokenback Ranges, the building evolved as a composition in silhouette, an ensemble of forms, approached in a processional manner via the newly established vines. We wanted to create a sense of ceremony upon arrival, it heightens the wine tasting experience," explains Walter.

Large-scale excavation was required to submerge the winemaking facility with the earthworks used to form a sloping landscape for the cellar door and associated restaurant and facilities.

This carving and shaping of the landscape provide the split below- and above-ground construction of the building to deliver an imposing and dramatic presence. "We wanted to capture the natural grandeur of the site in the building," says Walter.

The tasting room has been designed in the distinctive shape of a barrel, while the building also houses an underground winemaking cellar and the renowned fine-dining Muse restaurant. The circular structure of the cellar door implies industrial references and the tilted roof 'lid' brings natural sunlight into the spaces below.

Adjacent to the cellar-door drum is the restaurant and function facility, which complement the inward-looking drum with a steel-framed roof form that stands open and outward looking, capturing the views beyond.

The overall composition is anchored by an imposing stone chimney, which emerges from the large stone fireplace inside. There is a reinforcement of the architect's design intent to define a visual change of levels throughout the estate, from arrival to the ramped walkway that culminates in the cantilevered roof over the restaurant, framing the powerful mountain view.

"Hungerford Hill is a recognised, uniquely sculptural building, setting the scene for other winery establishments. The use of bold forms, rugged texture of the exterior, contrast with the warm, detailed interiors, with bespoke timber detailing and sandstone," says Walter.

Architecturally, the scale and drama have defined a sense of occasion at this landmark location, and the impressive space is now a destination cellar door and restaurant with an established reputation for premium wines and fine dining in the valley.

Walter Barda Design, which has been based in Sydney since 1987, offers consultancy services in planning, architecture, landscape and interior design. Within its diverse portfolio of work, Hungerford Hill stands out as a unique and rewarding challenge.

"Winery design is an interesting process where the architect needs to ensure winemakers and wine merchant all cohabit within a well-functioning layout. We enjoyed the creative process to deliver a unique addition to the Hunter Valley wine region," Walter says.

Running Horse
Hunter Valley

Thoroughbred design

A bold and intriguing vision of stacked, rustic shipping containers awaits travellers passing through the Hunter Valley and into the Broke Wine region.

Visitors to Running Horse are assured of a warm welcome from owner and ex-jockey David Fromberg, who combined a passion for horses and fine wines to create an unforgettable cellar door, enhanced by the close proximity of his thoroughbred stables.

Having lived on the site since 1988, Fromberg began making wine in 2000, three years before close friend and architect David Kaunitz of Kaunitz Yeung Architecture suggested he sell his produce commercially and build a cellar door.

"Running Horse vineyard is the labour of love built from scratch by David Fromberg and producing superb aged Hunter Valley wines," says Kaunitz.

Fromberg draws parallels between his two great passions by reflecting that, as in horse riding, it is what lies beneath you that is important for winemaking, because the structure of the vineyard soil ultimately determines the quality of the grape.

"Whether it's a thoroughbred or a grapevine, the forces of nature are equally challenging," says Fromberg, whose quality-over-quantity winemaking philosophy has delivered a range of aged wines that are as unique as the space that sells it.

Fromberg envisaged a two-storey structure that would capture both the distant views of Yellow Rock and the surrounding vineyards below. His vision finally became a reality in 2018 when Kaunitz designed a sustainable, iron-clad winery placed within the vineyard landscape. Fromberg was involved in every decision regarding the design and construction process, from the smallest detail to the overall height of the building forms, tailoring the concept to his specific requirements.

The resultant blending of industrial and agriculture structures forms a stunning visual relationship that can only deepen over time through the natural weathering of the façade materials. "When I thought about how the stacked shipping containers clad with weathering steel would look, I knew it would sit beautifully in that spot," says Fromberg.

Once commissioned, it did not take long for Kaunitz to sketch the designs and obtain council approval. However, constructing the unique concept proved challenging, given the difficulty in procuring a builder with relevant experience. A boilermaker was eventually appointed, who carefully welded the containers together at specific angels to ensure the cantilevered containers were structurally supported, as the project was completed on-site after a year.

"I wanted a welcoming space to give visitors a personal experience. It's not often that the winemaker themselves hosts the cellar door, so the building needed to reflect my down-to-earth approach to winemaking," recalls Fromberg. "This building and how it fits into the landscape are exactly what I'd hoped for. The proof is in the number of repeat customers who tell me how much they love the space and the reception they get here."

Fromberg describes being in his cellar door as a bit "like being in a treehouse. Every window you look out, there is a branch visible, and it creates a great natural experience."

There is no doubt in his mind that it is the striking architecture that makes people come and look at the building, and that once there don't feel the need to rush off, often staying for up to two hours.

Fromberg believes the difference between Running Horse and other cellar doors in the area is that visitors are more comfortable during the wine tasting because instead of facing someone behind a counter, they are able to look out across the vineyards while still interacting with fellow tasters.

External details of the construction and the balance of the sustainable and recycled materials on the terrain are complemented by the internal geometry of the containers, which frame the external vistas to form sweeping views best enjoyed with a glass of wine. The collaboration between the architect and client that created this unique cellar door certainly ensures a memorable wine-tasting environment that appeals to a wide range of visitors.

Montoro
Orange

Small but perfectly formed

Situated on the Cargo Road, in the cool climate of Orange in New South Wales, Montoro wines is a charming, enticing cellar door that has captured some of the most prestigious architecture awards in Australia.

As owners of a young boutique winery, conveniently positioned at the start of a well-established wine tasting route, Bob and Jennifer Derrick sought to create a more sophisticated cellar door than the archetypal tin sheds dominating the region.

After purchasing the rundown vineyard in 2008, the Derricks spent three years rehabilitating the vines, producing a small vintage in 2010. The first commercial vintage was 2013 Montoro Pepper Shiraz, which went on to win several gold medals and be rated New South Wales' best mature red wine in 2018.

"Our licence was for mail and electronic orders and this served us well for a number of years until people started knocking on our windows and doors looking for a tasting cellar door. It was then that we started planning for the Montoro cellar door," they recall.

The planning brief included energy-neutral construction, utilisation of the valley views, visual appeal from the road, and most importantly, a wow factor, while the choice of architect followed a fortuitous turn of events.

"We just so happened to pass Source Architects, which had just set up their business in Orange, and drop in one day. They were not one of the three firms on our original list, but from our very first meeting we were enthusiastic, as were Sally and David Sutherland, and when we saw their concepts and the reasoning behind their ideas, we looked no further," the Derricks explain.

"The original brief we received in September 2016 was for a small shed-style cellar door where Montoro could hold tastings and sell their wine. A key requirement was that it needed to be open for Orange Wine Week in October the following year, which gave us just over a year from start to finish for the project, which is pretty tight," remembers David. "The owners were also keen to create an element that was obvious from the road so resolving these contradictory elements was a key consideration in the design."

Their solution was to cap the 'little jewel of a tasting room' with an oversized canopy roof, sitting in a field of native grasses and wildflowers, that provided a stunning statement from the road. The sculptural black timber–clad wall forms a continuous link between inside and outside, introducing visitors into the wine-tasting room and views beyond. It divides the internal space from service to administration areas, while acting as a barrier to the external road and strong winds.

Bob is proud of the innovative construction of the prefabricated elements off-site and the way the services are integrated, such as connecting the electricity underground without detracting from the beauty and symmetry of the standalone building.

Though the oversized roofing material proved a challenge to deliver to the site, the resultant overhead form provides a desirable presence and identity in its setting. The distinctive cellar door quickly become a local talking point while drawing in many a passing driver.

At almost 30 metres (98 feet) in length, the canopy roof provides a visual statement; not only is it large enough to cover the entry sequence and internal spaces, it cantilevers over the terrace as a sunshade.

The cosy tasting space enables a more personalised wine-tasting experience, where the owners greet all visitors and the orientation of the building platform provides compelling landscape settings for each of the four seasons. The building is oriented to capture the expansive views to the north and north-west, and the all-important northern light. Despite the external climate, the interior space is warm, welcoming and calm, as the steel-and-glass structure captures the winter sun while keeping the building pleasantly cool in summer.

According to the architect, "The layout seeks to encourage patrons to linger, to take up residence for the afternoon on the terrace or to sit on the edge of the platform and talk while kids play in the field beyond, and to generally be a part of the beautiful landscape that the building is sharing."

Bob and Jennifer believe the architecture enhances wine tasting by providing a modern and well-lit open environment where external colours shift continually as the sun sets.

Their enthusiasm is shared by the architecture community, with the cellar door winning a NSW State Architecture Award and securing the top prize, the James Barnet Award, at the prestigious Australian Institute of Architects' NSW Country Division Awards in 2018.

The jury of experts also awarded Montoro its trophy for commercial architecture, noting: "The design is simple and elegant. Small yet robust, it sits neatly in its setting of native grasses and open fields, providing a vantage point to survey the surrounding landscape."

David believes, "Simply, the space is a pleasure to be in, and to drink wine in and is rapidly becoming a favourite with locals for a lazy Sunday afternoon."

Logan
Mudgee

Through the looking glass

Small independent winemaker Peter Logan purchased the eponymously named estate a quarter of a century ago in the then little-known NSW Central Ranges, with the simple aspiration of making wine he liked to drink.

The winery is the first one visitors encounter on trips from Sydney, and the last stop when leaving the now booming food and wine destination of Mudgee, once one of Australia's best kept secrets.

Mudgee, the birthplace of Australian Chardonnay, is said to mean 'nest in the hills' in the local Wiradjuri Aboriginal dialect. The combination of soils, sites and climates are ideal for creating a variety of wines of depth and character.

Despite what he was taught at wine college and what the establishment was doing, Peter planted Tempranillo, and made Pinot Gris and Gewürztraminer, employing different winemaking methods including fermenting white grapes on their skins, using large barrel oak and wild yeasts, and then selling his wine in kegs.

Further to previous work he had undertaken with the Logans, architect Stephen Buzacott commenced the design of the cellar door in 2003, one that would accommodate a tasting room, sales, and office and service spaces. "The building had to be contemporary, memorable and have a presence in the landscape," Peter recalls. The resultant Logan cellar door is a modern tasting room, perched above the vines in a cantilevered box, with views over the vineyard and Apple Tree Flat. Here the wines are perfectly matched with stunning surroundings that enhance a guided and seated tasting experience that is proudly outward looking.

Initially, a barrel room was proposed to be located under the main building to minimise the footprint, thereby creating a large outdoor terrace area above, and although the barrel room was not included in the final design, the original design intent was retained.

"The building, set high above the road on the hillside then sat on a plinth, which increased the scale of the building while limiting its impact. The use of a masonry base gives the building an air of an Italian country villa," Stephen explains.

"Before deciding on a site we looked at four site options, two closer to the road, one on the other side of the highway adjacent the Cudgegong River and the current site," he says. "The site further up the hill allowed a longer entry sequence, winding up and around the building to enter from behind. This allows for visitors to 'decompress' after the long car journey from Sydney and good views up to the building."

Travellers arrive at the 'rear' solid masonry wall and then proceed though the spaces to the glazed light-filled room.

Stephen describes this sense of arrival at the wine-tasting destination: "The skillion roof allows highlights over the sales counter that gives views up to the treed ridge behind giving the sense of the building surrounded by the large landscape." He says, "The long tasting room projects out into the landscape giving views over the vineyards adjacent. The large terrace allows visitors to be both 'in' the building and 'in' the landscape, and acts like a traditional belvedere."

The Logan brand is complemented by the modern design, whereby the architecture responds to the surrounding landscape. There is also a sense of tradition in the high ceilings and tall chimney, which in turn aims to express the wine industry itself. The three spaces that offer wine-tasting experiences are the tasting room, the projecting glazed lounge area and the large open terrace, all seamlessly connected with a wide external eaves providing solar shading.

"The beautiful bucolic setting of Mudgee, also my home, with its rolling hills, Cudgegong River and green farm lands is impressed upon you when you are sitting on the deck of our tasting room," states Peter.

"At the time, the Logan cellar door stood out as the only contemporary cellar-door design in the Mudgee wine region," Stephen recalls. "It needed to stand out and say something about the brand." Since the building was completed, it retains its presence in the landscape with an uncluttered approach, and a timeless and sophisticated design.

Visitors still ask Peter how long the building has been here and are surprised when he tells them 15 years. "They were thinking it's brand new," he proudly declares.

Amelia Park
Margaret River

Evolutionary design

Located in the heart of Margaret River, one of Western Australia's foremost winemaking regions, Amelia Park makes judicious use of beautiful natural surrounds, and ideal soil and weather conditions.

Multi-award-winning winemaker Jeremy Gordon, assisted by wife Daniela and business partner Peter Walsh, has helped elevate Amelia Park into the top 5 percent of wineries in Australia since launching in 2009.

Building upon the winery's well-established reputation for quality wines and progressive approach to the industry, the trio embarked on the next evolutionary step – the construction of a quality winemaking facility and cellar door that thoughtfully reflect the excellence of the final product.

The three envisaged the cellar door echoing what happens in the winery with an elegant and refined approach, using formal materials such as concrete, wood and steel, forming strong lines, and creating spaces people can connect with.

Capturing the views over the gorgeous vineyards during wine tasting was a design priority, while creating something true to the Amelia Park brand values of tradition, craft and quality was another key goal.

Architect Beth Courtney of Courtico Design + Architecture, who has known Daniela and Jeremy since they were teenagers, helped turn their vision into a modern, stylish and captivating reality.

"For the winemaking client, function comes first in winery design, but the cellar-door experience can be crucial to the brand of the winery and the sales made at the cellar door," Beth emphasizes.

Beth was presented with a brief to create a master plan that catered for the large-scale function of the winery, and design a cellar-door building that was to become the interface for Amelia Park to all visitors to the region.

The initial sketch design concept involved a series of walls of varying lengths and heights that formed the basis for the architecture and landscape. These elements were positioned to take full advantage of the views, cater for the slope of the land and control the differences in scales of buildings required on-site. Some of the walls

formed horizontal ramps and others the vertical sides to structures. The concept allowed for future expansion as Amelia Park grew and changed, while retaining the original design ideas.

The winery itself was built to Jeremy's specification, based on his years of winemaking experience. The brief was mindful of reducing energy and water consumption, and the need to maximise gravity where possible to limit its impact on the wine.

"We hope that our space captures the essence of our brand and brings people an exceptional tasting experience to go with our exceptional wines," says Daniela.

The final design differentiates itself from other wineries in the area in the way the architecture controls how the winery is revealed. The large solid front door establishes an intriguing entrance that leads to a windowless barrel room. Further, beyond wooden doors, is the cellar-door tasting room, where the space dramatically opens up as the architecture delivers both a prescribed journey and rewarding destination.

"I like to think we bring an experiential tasting experience to our visitors. From driving into the property and looking out over the vineyards to walking through our cellar-door barrel room before entering our tasting area, which has gorgeous views over the Wilyabrup Valley – the heart of Margaret River," Daniela opines.

Each space is designed to elevate the senses, allowing patrons to be immersed in the wine experience, travelling along an exploration path to the finished bottled wine product with the best vision saved for last.

"To take full advantage of the site and all it has to offer, the best view was revealed over time. As you proceed through the cellar-door building, which is very enclosed, you then feel the release as you reach the end of the building and the large windows open up to the magnificent view," Beth says.

Gracing the cover of *Gourmet Traveller WINE* as winner of its Star Cellar Door Award for the Margaret River Region three years in a row (2017–19) is an honour that acknowledges the creation of a beautiful space to taste the Amelia Park wines. "Enjoy striking views over the Wilyabrup Valley at a visual masterpiece of a building, all maximising the tasting experience. Already superb wines will get even better with the leadership of talented winemaker Jeremy Gordon," the awards panel stated.

Leeuwin Estate
Margaret River

The art of fine wine

Still affectionately known within the family as 'the farm', Leeuwin Estate, established by Denis and Tricia Horgan in 1973, has grown from humble beginnings into an internationally lauded winery and home to an award-winning restaurant, renowned art gallery and concert venue.

The fifth winery founded in the Margaret River district of Western Australia, Leeuwin Estate was built on land previously used as a cattle farm but identified by legendary Napa Valley winemaker Robert Mondavi as ideal for the production of premium wine.

Perth-based chartered accountant Denis took up the challenge after having acquired the land as part of his purchase of a plumbing business in 1969. Four years later the site was being transformed into a vineyard, driven by a mission statement "to produce wines that rank with the best in the world through the pursuit of excellence". The winery was opened in 1978.

Day-to-day running of the business has now been handed over to the oldest Horgan children, Simone and Justin, who, together with siblings Rebecca and Christian and a third generation comprising nine cousins, have maintained the family's passion for the property and Margaret River.

Suzanne Hunt Architect's principal, Suzie Hunt, had worked closely with the family for over 15 years, providing architectural and interior design advice on several prior projects, and was approached in 2015 to discuss their thoughts about some new work.

According to Suzie, "Anyone that works with the Horgans are embraced as part of their extended family including myself, my practice and my children." They are wonderfully loyal clients and "the best advocates an architectural practice could ever ask for".

Simone Furlong worked closely with the Suzanne Hunt Architect team to establish the design vision and realistic expectations of the new works. "We decided to create a master plan for a comprehensive restoration and refurbishment of Leeuwin Estate's front-of-house hospitality spaces." Simone notes that Suzie "understood our vision to respect the original winery architecture as we revitalised the building." Her previous

experience at the winery gave her an insight into the brief's requirements, and while she recognised the constraints in the existing buildings, she could also visualise the amazing opportunities. Suzie felt that the clients trusted and respected her, so it was really important that she was honest with them. A holistic approach to a long-term master plan was recommended, with a comprehensive scope of work that included maintenance and repair as well as a contemporary refurbishment and new work.

The main building was designed by Tony Ednie-Brown in the 1970s, and over the years the original design intent became lost in the continuing additions required to meet the demands of a flourishing winemaking company. The estate buildings had become tired looking and dated, and were not compatible with the winery's reputation.

Suzanne Hunt Architect's masterplan design for a complex and ambitious refurbishment aimed to streamline the winery processes and preserve heritage structures, "without sacrificing the quirkiness of spaces over its 50-year history so the winery could thrive for another 50 years or more."

Simone and her family were keen to treat the project as a heritage restoration, transforming original spaces for contemporary use and bringing back to life materials that had faded over time. She notes: "It was important to us to remain true to our foundations and maintain the essence of what generations of visitors have enjoyed about Leeuwin Estate."

The works comprised a healthy overhaul that still celebrated the architectural and interior character of the original buildings, utilising principles of sustainability through reusing, recycling and repurposing structures and materials.

The transformation of the iconic winery also aimed to increase functionality and profitability with new additions, including a spectacular frameless glass roof for the verandah restaurant, refurbishment of the ground-floor space to improve the food and beverage on offer, and the creation of a state-of-the-art gallery in the original barrel room downstairs.

The architect's brief was to transform this cellar space into a light-filled, acoustically sound art gallery to showcase the Australian artworks that have featured on the labels of Leeuwin Estate's famed 'Art Series' wines since 1981. This spectacular collection of contemporary Australian art now comprises more than 180 paintings from the country's finest artists, including John Olsen, Arthur Boyd and Sir Sidney Nolan, which are rotated through the gallery and restaurant for visitors to enjoy.

The architecture of the winery allows separate spaces for those wishing to dine, taste wine or view the art and overlook the natural amphitheatre where the annual summertime Leeuwin Concert series is staged.

Simone believes "the building has successfully repurposed spaces for contemporary use and incorporated the beauty of the natural environment into visitors' experiences." Her favourite part of the winery is the restaurant verandah, where you can enjoy a long lunch, seated under the new steel-and-glass pergola laden with wisteria vines, with the karri forest in the background.

According to Suzie Hunt, "The architecture is deliberately quiet and low-key, respectfully playing a supporting role" to the high-quality food and wine, art and music on offer at Leeuwin. As a destination much loved by its loyal clientele from around the world, it was important to ensure they still felt at home here.

Passel Estate
Margaret River

Rehabilitation and conservatism

Passel Estate offers a joyous, life-affirming wine-tasting experience within a tranquil Margaret River bush setting that fully embraces the owners' support and protection of local wildlife.

Owners Wendy and Barry Stimpson, who originate from England and South Africa, respectively, made Margaret River their home in 2005, having been awed by the region's pristine natural environment and world-class wines during numerous preceding visits.

"We fell in love with the property from the moment we walked on it – it was a purchase of pure emotion," the couple reminisce.

It remains a sanctuary for threatened fauna, with the winery's timber form suggesting a subtle nod to the original possum boxes located throughout the property. "Passel Estate has a real commitment to nature rehabilitation and conservation. It is home to a number of endangered species within its natural bushland including a family (or passel) of critically endangered western ringtail possums, which have been reintroduced to the estate and inspired the name," Wendy explains.

Wendy and Barry engaged local architect Theo Mathews to design the cellar-door tasting room and sales building, further to a successful collaboration on their home a few years earlier. They requested a modest venue that would best showcase the excellence of their wines, while emphasising the importance of the sanctuary and its stunning surrounds. "The building was envisioned by the clients and myself as a sculptural piece – a jewel that sits comfortably and complements the setting," Theo says.

The resultant structure was strongly influenced by the site orientation, vineyard and bushland context. Its lakeside location provides the desired outlook across the water, as both the uplifting roof form and full-height glazing meet the visibility and natural-light requirements. A stone wall anchors the tasting room, which has been constructed using materials sourced from the estate wherever possible. The owners particularly love

this part of the winery, which was painstakingly crafted by a local stonemason using the granite rocks unearthed when preparing to plant a new Chardonnay vineyard.

Wendy says that "the architects' sensitive incorporation of the stone wall internally and externally represents a stunning architectural feature that lends understated elegance, warmth and balance to the contemporary design of the tasting room."

Theo emphasises how the architecture enhances the winery experience. "It features floor-to-ceiling glass on three sides so that visitors are immediately connected with the surrounding vines and bushland conservation sanctuary, which are integral to the winery's story," he says. "Stone walls and stunning timbers are used throughout, sourced from the estate wherever possible."

Passel differs from other wineries in the Margaret River region, not only through its small scale, but also its integration and commitment to nature rehabilitation and conservation. In addition to the traditional wine-tasting and quality architecture experience, guests are encouraged to take nature and wine walks or spend a morning planting native tube stocks to help create an ideal environment for the estate's namesake.

Wendy firmly believes the architecture contributes to the destination. "The building is beautifully appointed and sets the scene for a unique, high end and wholly authentic wine tasting experience. Many of our visitors are drive-by, who turn in initially because they are struck by the beauty of the building and the setting."

Margaret River

Vasse Felix
Margaret River

The lucky vineyard

Established in 1967 as Margaret River's founding wine estate, Vasse Felix has broadened its regional leadership credentials through a series of progressive expansions, culminating in the creation of an acclaimed multi-purpose cellar door.

The estate is intriguingly named after Thomas Timothée Vasse, an assistant helmsman who was swept overboard on a French ship's maiden trip to the south-west coast of Australia in 1801. Legend has it he was then either imprisoned by the English, drowned or washed ashore. Estate founder, Tom Cullity, an avid historian, hoped his vineyard would enjoy a happier fate than the unfortunate seaman and decided to name it Vasse Felix, which translates as 'lucky/happy' Vasse.

A long-term vision to build a great wine estate of the world in Margaret River naturally led to the architectural and interior redevelopment of the cellar door, featuring new ancillary areas.

The transformation was undertaken by Perth-based architects Iredale Pedersen Hook in collaboration with Melbourne interior designers Hecker Guthrie, and was managed by Lloyd Constantine, sales and marketing manager at Vasse Felix.

Lloyd recalls, "Our definition of a great cellar-door experience incorporated a number of tasting spaces (formal to informal), restaurant, art gallery, wine lounge and underground cellar and museum."

The brief was to create a timeless, creative and unique space, and to deliver the Vasse Felix brand positioning. They envisioned a "beautifully bespoke design with attention to detail, incorporating handcrafted elements and sold materials designed to last indefinitely".

Hamish Guthrie at Hecker Guthrie understood that the design needed to 'reflect the treasured heritage and family ownership of the brand'. Their design vision was developed as 'raw to refined', inspired by the ruggedness of the landscape and the refinement of the Vasse Felix food and wine production.

Lloyd considered their concept 'brilliant' and the big ideas 'going dark, the theatre of display, neon highlights, the Margaret River narrative, and signage' celebrated the activities in the winery.

Margaret River

The interior spaces incorporate contemporary joinery, furniture and lighting to both complement and contrast the original 1970s architecture. Local raw materials such as granite stone, jarrah wood and bespoke fittings and custom-made joinery created a beautiful, refined edge. Even beams from the original Busselton Jetty, which was destroyed by Cyclone Alby in 1978, were incorporated in the winery design. Hamish notes, "The interior pays homage to the skill and craftsmanship of the existing building by favouring authentic finishes and furniture produced by local craftspeople and artisans."

Architects Iredale Pedersen Hook worked in association with the interior designers to transform the iconic winery and cellar door into a cohesive and memorable landmark for the region. Over several years, the architects had tactfully stripped back years of accumulated additions and modifications in a methodical and deliberate process. They were able to present the authentic and original endearing qualities of the existing architecture in terms of its generous volumes, tactile material palette and spectacular views.

The architects redefined the circulation and connectivity between spaces with new insertions to the existing building envelope, and the new links make it "difficult to see where the existing stops and the new begins".

The synergy between Iredale Pederson Hook's additions and Hecker Guthrie's interiors allows the winery to address the vineyard from any vantage and operate in a more functional and engaged position. The various spaces within the estate allow for a range of formal and informal wine-tasting experiences, and they empower the visitor to experience the wines in the manner most preferable to themselves.

One of the many redesigned spaces is the 'Vault', an underground museum that is undoubtably the owner's favourite part of the winery. It is intimate, dramatic and beautiful, and it reflects the history and investment required to make the wines.

Concrete and steel stairs descend to a dark and theatrical undercroft where the pedigree, heritage and history of Vasse Felix are showcased. The concrete floor, blackened ceiling, dark joinery and dimmed lighting seem to compress this spatial volume. "Everything has dropped to a black," Hamish says. "This move immerses visitors in the space and allows the wine to cut through and become the focal point."

According to Lloyd, "The design process was fuelled by fine wine and passionate people and reflective of the premier wine destination on offer here at Vasse Felix." And Hamish learnt that "there is plenty to talk about on a 3-hour road trip from Perth to Margaret River."

Lloyd surmises that "it is important that the architecture complements the overall experience when tasting and enjoying wine. Wine is an all-encompassing sensory experience and as such the surrounds should enhance this, as well as match the quality of the wine."

Overall, the architecture and interior design interventions adapt the history of Vasse Felix to a contemporary context, creating a place that is unique and in harmony with the natural environment of Margaret River.

Domaine Chandon
Yarra Valley

Sparkling destination

Australia's only sparkling-wine producer with genuine French heritage, Domaine Chandon was established in 1986 as part of the pioneering vision and thirst for new lands set out by the Chandon Australia founder, Robert-Jean de Vogüé.

Following an initial overseas planting in Mendoza, Argentina, in 1959, Robert-Jean collaborated with Californian entrepreneur John Wright to create the celebrated Napa Valley estate in 1973, the same year a Brazilian subsidiary was founded in the foothills of the Serra Gaucha mountains.

The cool climate and great soil of an old Green Point dairy farm in Victoria's Yarra Valley was subsequently identified as the ideal location for the brand's expansion into new territories.

To celebrate its sparkling wines crafted with a distinct French style and Australian expertise, Domaine Chandon – as part of the global Möet Hennessy luxury wines and spirits division of LVMH – rejuvenated the cellar door in 2017 to create a new brand immersion across the tasting bar, dining and retail spaces. The original Homestead was meticulously and lovingly restored, while the cellar-door building from the 1980s was transformed into a stunning space that provides a direct connection to the vineyards.

Foolscap Studio, an award-winning interior architecture and design practice, was appointed to design and deliver the works in less than 12 months. Inspired by the ritual of popping the cork on a bottle of bubbles, they created spaces that spontaneously celebrate heritage with a twenty-first-century radiance. The volume and vaulted ceiling of the existing structure were retained, while the interior architecture treatment was integrated through a series of bold gestures.

"We've done this by blending three distinct taste experiences – cellar door, hospitality and a dedicated 'by-the-glass' lounge, featuring a centralised banquette coupled with a playful, bubble-inspired kinetic mobile to embody the feeling of buoyancy," explains Adèle Winteridge, director at Foolscap Studio.

Views of the surrounding vineyards provided a natural starting point to consider the visitor experience, with the application of colour throughout serving to reflect

the shifting seasonal tones. "The hospitality centre offers access to the best views in the Yarra Valley – of the estate and vineyards and mountains beyond, so it was important to draw on the colours in the landscape to unify the interior and exterior elements," Adèle says. The idea of alchemy was fundamental to Foolscap's conceptual approach, with different metals and finish treatments applied throughout.

The process of transformation in winemaking also informed the design of each space where compression/release is revealed in the enclosed, intimate tasting room and the airy/exuberant zone is evident in the open lounge bar, according to Adèle. The duality of density and lightness in sparkling wine is alluded to in the juxtaposition of solid, opaque substances with open-woven materials. These ideas have been rendered in a style that is respectful of the tradition of the brand yet indicate a youthfulness due to its relatively recent establishment within its lineage. For example, there is international inspiration seen in the Parisian aesthetic with the brass light fittings and leather upholstered banquettes, while at the same time, local materials are incorporated to add character.

"Using Australian sourced materials was key in creating a warm, elegant environment that celebrates the setting and enhances the experience," Adèle notes. "We've used native spotted gum timber, textiles designed by Indigenous artists and Queensland marble to give Chandon Australia its own luxurious and local identity."

The retail space was a critical component in resolution of the brief, and central to the design and layout of the interior architecture scheme. Foolscap worked closely with local craftspeople and manufacturers to realise their ideas and showcase the products in a creative setting that elevates the retail experience, with unique and dynamic displays.

In addition to a range of wine-tasting and dining options with a subtle French twist, visitors can experience the Chandon Sunday School, which takes them behind the scenes "to discover how 250 years of Champagne history and Australian expertise goes into every bottle of Chandon sparkling wine".

Adèle claims, "Chandon is about celebrating life with friends and family. We wanted to create an atmosphere that was casual, unpretentious and fun, while at the same time, refined and elegant." Foolscap Studio has succeeded in delivering this vision and created a design well worth drinking to.

Levantine Hill
Yarra Valley

The grand masterplan

A luxury wine estate in the heart of the Yarra Valley, Levantine Hill was established in 2010 by Lebanese-born property developer turned wine creator Elias Jreissati, whose family has a long history of grape growing in the Middle East.

High-quality wines are produced from two divergent vineyards, the first of which is located on a hill originally deemed by experts to be too steep with too many underlying rocks to plant viable vines. Elias was nevertheless determined to exploit the plot's 'perfect' soil profile and, after removing the rocks with a diamond-tipped drilling rig, set out to secure a reputation for delivering only premium wines in high-quality vintages.

This vineyard producing superior grapes was subsequently merged with individual family blocks or paddocks, which surround the homestead and are named after wife Colleen and daughters Samantha, Melissa and Katherine.

The 62-hectare (153-acre) estate comprises two parcels of land, both an hour's drive from Melbourne, and has grown to incorporate a restaurant, a cellar door and a new winery complex in addition to the celebrated vineyards. The building that houses a signature restaurant with a Mediterranean-inspired menu, all-day dining space and cellar door was designed by Australian architects Fender Katsalidis and completed in 2015.

Karl Fender OAM, is a close friend of the Jreissati family, having previously worked with them through their development company, Bensons Property Group, on numerous major residential projects. He was given free rein to help them realise the project that remains very close to their hearts. "Our client's aspiration was to create the finest quality Australian wines that would be highly appreciated both nationally and internationally," Karl recalls. "In addition, they felt the need to equally reflect their commitment to design excellence in the new buildings with a sensitive, interpretive architecture that clearly demonstrated their passion for the beauty of the Yarra Valley."

Sharing the family's obsession with perfection, Karl's concept was to design a place that would be appropriate and sit sensitively within the rural setting. Inspired by its winemaking purpose, he designed curved forms that evoke the impression of a huge

barrel resting on the ground, and echo and blend into the surrounding undulating landscape. "The architectural solutions incorporated at Levantine Hill Estate were considered to be extremely important. The two buildings completed to date contrive to provide an uplifting rural and wine experience in spaces and places that are quite unusual, unexpected and exciting," Karl notes.

The cellar-door exterior features exposed black steel, curved metal roofing, expansive glazing and apricot-coloured timber. Internally, within the uninterrupted vaulted ceiling, there are barrel-style tasting booths that frame picturesque vistas in an intimate setting. Exposed raw concrete, raw and precious metals, and expressed Australian hardwood timbers have been selected to reflect the cultivated natural surroundings.

A clear master plan that considers operational, contextual and tourism perspectives has been developed as a result of a thoughtful and collaborative process involving all stakeholders. A detailed brief evolved in stages, which laid out the locations of the wine varieties, the production facilities, the cellar door and guest accommodation. It was envisioned to create an environment around mentoring people about wine production, winemaking and overall wine appreciation.

The next stage for the estate is the new winery complex, which is nearing completion. Positioned near the main highway approach to be clear, convenient

destination landmarks, the roof forms are curved, with a powerful barrel-vault form to the winery. According to the architect, "the visual combination of the two buildings is intended to signal a potentially amazing wine experience".

"We wanted the winery to make a global statement from the Yarra Valley, and to continue to elevate the region as a world-class producer of fine wines – and architecture," says Levantine Hill managing director Samantha Jreissati. "The form had to be grand and sculptural in nature. We also wanted to use materials that fit the environment – like natural galvanized-steel purlins and corrugated-iron cladding, which reflect the cultivated natural surroundings."

Karl has created an embassy for the brand and the new sculptural building complements his adjacent existing design, as well as aspiring to benchmark Levantine Hill against the best in the world. The sheer ambition and scale of the soaring façade will be defined against the landscape, and an underground barrel store will serve as an immersive backdrop to any wine-tasting experience. "You will find yourself wondering if you are in the Yarra Valley or the south of France," Samantha suggests. "This world-class building is truly a work of art and will bring visitors from all corners of the globe to taste our wines and experience the architecture."

Ultimately, what makes this winery different from other wineries in the region is the clear dedication to its architecture, matched so perfectly with its approach to wine, and the mission to create an unforgettable, sensory experience for all guests at Levantine Hill.

Yarra Valley

Medhurst
Yarra Valley

Family dream

The captivating Medhurst estate represents the realisation of a long-held and shared dream for husband-and-wife team Ross and Robyn Wilson to own a vineyard property within the renowned Yarra Valley wine region where Robyn spent her childhood.

A former CEO of Southcorp, which acquired Penfolds, Lyndemans and Wynns in 1990, Ross retained his passion for wine as he and Robyn searched for the perfect site to create their own high-quality vintages.

After years of looking for a suitable property, in 2000 they planted vines at Medhurst, chosen for its favourable microclimate, north-facing slopes, good drainage and excellent aspect to proudly deliver "estate-grown, handmade wines that are a pure expression of site and season".

In 2019 Medhurst's cellar-door extension was completed, positioned on the hill overlooking the vineyard, providing a clear connection with the surrounding landscape.

The owners' brief had been for a cellar door that "both complements our passion for making the best possible wines from the Medhurst vineyard while providing visitors with a welcoming and memorable experience. In our view the building achieves both of these objectives."

"The new extension and tasting area serve as a welcome meeting place and we love the way elements of the original cellar door have been reused in the design. We are thrilled with the positive response from both regular and new patrons."

Folk Architects was engaged to undertake the works and sought to "expand the tasting experience and address the site in a broader context," according to directors Tim Wilson and Christie Petsinis. "Through masterplanning, site analysis and extensive consultation with the client, it was established that a linear extension to the existing building was an effective intervention," they recall.

The resultant design is a pavilion orientated to the north with full-height curved glazing towards the views, and solid cladding anchoring the south of the building. The internal open plan allows for flexible spaces including tasting areas, restaurant,

function space and retail offerings. Raw and natural materials have been incorporated in the interior design to accentuate the sights and smells associated with winemaking, enhance the tasting experience and reference the Australian bush. "The design approach reinforces the experience of discovering the architecture within the vineyard and bush setting. Providing a spatial hierarchy while framing key views to the surrounding context, the formal language of the buildings' volumes link the cellar door with the winery that sits adjacent," describes Tim.

The decision to build a new winery on the site in 2010 was driven by the requirement to have complete control over the product, and the ability to utilise small-batch processing that would enhance the quality of the wines.

Medhurst was impressed by Folk Architects' initial pitch, which met the brief for a flexible winery building that was sympathetic to the existing property and took advantage of the site topography.

Winemaker Simon Steel notes, "The Folk Architects trademark seems to be flow. Not only in the design of our winery here at Medhurst, but also the ease of use as a winemaking facility of the highest order. Overall, it's a pleasure to work in the space and the wines themselves benefit greatly by having been cared for in a timely, efficient manner and at optimal temperatures for creating fine wines."

The state-of-the-art winery features an underground barrel storage and is embedded within the hillside setting, minimising energy needed for cooling. After assessing different sites on the property, and considering the practical requirements, it was chosen for providing the opportunity to integrate the natural surroundings with the winemaking process. The architects' response was to "camouflage the building into the Warramate Hill, as a means to reduce its visual impact on the surrounding landscape."

"The building was conceived as an installation rather than a solid built form – a series of horizontal lines follow the contours of the site. When overlooked from the cellar door and its southern approach, the building is predominantly nestled into the hill, framing views to the vineyard and across the Yarra Valley beyond."

A meandering path leads patrons from wine tasting in the cellar door to an elevated green roof platform, situated above the subterranean barrel hall, with visual links to both the surrounding vines and production area. "As we became increasingly interested in winemaking, our intention to enable public engagement in this process was added to the design brief. Visual permeability to fermenters, tanks and equipment is complementary to Medhurst's cellar door, and adds to the experience of visiting the Yarra Valley wine region," recalls Tim.

The client and users are delighted with their new facility – notably, the permeability between functional and public areas, the deceptive scale and integration of the building into its surroundings.

In terms of the architectural contribution to the winery destination, Tim and Christie agree, "Commercially, wineries rely upon cellar door and visitation to be viable businesses. From a patron's perspective, having a relationship with a place creates an experience and an education on the product adds to their appreciation for fine wine. In this sense, our work needs to be pragmatic yet create a memorable and enjoyable experience for people to engage and be encouraged to understand more about the product and process."

Oakridge
Yarra Valley

A bold red

An hour's drive from Melbourne, in the epicentre of the Yarra Valley grape-growing community, Oakridge has evolved into a must-visit regional destination, famous for a dramatic reception building as much as its award-sweeping collection of wines.

Oakridge has been making wine in the region since its founding in 1978, initially at Seville and then at Coldstream where it relocated 20 years later, before being acquired in 2007 by the D'Aloisio-Atlas family. The family shared a vision to develop the estate into a top fine-wine producer and quality food offering, built on a farm to plate local produce.

Traditional winemaking methods, minimal intervention and meticulous expertise create carefully crafted wines, that are known for their elegance and subtlety, and provide perfect companionship to food. The philosophy behind the wine is to leave a lasting impression of great wine that begins in the vineyard.

This excellence has been affirmed by an impressive tally of wine and food awards, including being voted Australian Winery of the Year in *The Age & Sydney Morning Herald Good Wine Guide* in 2012.

Reflective of the estate's winemaking prowess, the owners planned and delivered a visually stunning and practical cellar door, restaurant and function space, which opened its doors to the public to considerable acclaim in 2013.

They saw the need for a venue to complement the wine and food that "was itself a place people wished to visit for its architecture in the vines," recalls Tony D'Aloisio AM, director and owner of Oakridge Estate.

Denton Corker Marshall was approached to undertake the architectural design, which involved the demolition of an existing building to create space for the new cellar door and a flexible dining area. John Denton had designed two other projects in the region and offered what the winery wanted in terms of the clean lines, simplicity and quality of design.

"We were looking for contemporary and modern architecture which invited interest to visit and then enter and then when inside presented the full panorama of the Yarra Valley and vineyards," remembers Ilana Atlas AO, director and owner of Oakridge Estate.

The design vision was developed after extensive research by the owners on wine architecture in other regions in Australia, as well as in France, Spain and the Napa Valley in the United States.

The brief included the requirement for a function space that could accommodate over 100 people, and this was realised through the ability to convert the restaurant when needed. In order to continue operating during construction, the project was staged in two parts. The resultant building design has a distinctive form with a red cantilevered box sitting on top of the single-level spaces, which is highly visible from the highway approach.

According to the architects, "The floating red stick entices clientele to visit, highlights the Oakridge brand and acts as a wayfinding device to orientate visitors from arrival through to the cellar door and restaurant." As well as identifying the winery destination, it acts as an undercover entry, leading from the car park to the entrance. The clever design of the red box also houses all of the services equipment, allowing for full-height floor-to-ceiling glazing in both spaces at ground level. "Internally the experience is all about the view. The cellar door is arranged so that guests can view the vineyards and Yarra Valley beyond through large floor-to-ceiling glass windows, while they undertake tastings," emphasises Denton Corker Marshall. "Likewise, the restaurant is orientated to the view with a simplicity and clarity of design, aimed to focus the visitor on the vineyard, the wine and the food."

The cellar door and restaurant are housed in two separate boxes, divided by an external courtyard that contains a majestic oak tree. The importance of site and location in the design aim to reinforce the Oakridge brand, and pay homage to the row of oak trees along the estate after which the winery was named.

Cellar-door tastings are available for all group sizes and a diverse wine portfolio can be enjoyed, including easy-drinking and more premium wines. In keeping with the brand's family values, three areas are named after the owners' grandchildren: Gus's Courtyard, Will's Wine Room and Maggie's Tasting Room. "Naturally our favourite spots!" Tony claims.

A vibrant kitchen garden at the back of the property supplies most of the ingredients for the restaurant menu, where the head chefs are committed to sustainable and hyperlocal cooking philosophies. The estate's kitchen and vineyard crew created the Oakridge garden, and vintage pressings are used for its sustenance and growth.

Overall, the composition of the distinctive rectilinear forms provides a counterpoint to the undulating hills and oak trees. Ilana notes, "The building is an integral part of the Oakridge experience, anchored in wine and food and service in a spectacular setting."

The diverse Yarra Valley region consists of more than 80 wineries, and while each has its own offering and vibrancy, the red cantilever at Oakridge literally stands out, leaving a distinctive and lasting impression, much like its wine.

TarraWarra
Yarra Valley

Ground-breaking design

A love of both Burgundy wines and adopted country encapsulates the story of TarraWarra estate, which began in 1979 when Marc Besen and wife Eva purchased the property, initially as a family retreat. Four years later, with encouragement and guidance from local Yarra Valley winemaking legend Dr John Middleton, the Besens planted the first 6 hectares (14.8 acres) of Chardonnay and Pinot Noir. Forty years on, the now 400-hectare (988-acre) estate includes 28 hectares (69 acres) of vines, an extensive nature reserve, cattle grazing, kitchen garden, museum of art, and stunning cellar door and restaurant, which visitors are encouraged to explore and enjoy. "From the outset, our vision has been to produce wines of great quality and integrity amid a location of beauty and welcome. It is a vision created to be shared," the couple say.

The Besens' ambitious and colourful journey, driven by Marc's gratitude to a country that welcomed him to its shores in 1947, has been enhanced through the construction of a beguiling subterranean cellar door that fulfils the architect's and client's playful vision, 'like Alice down the rabbit hole'.

With the previous cellar door and restaurant space no longer meeting the needs of an expanding visitor base, the client brief focused on the idea of an extended barrel hall that connected to a dedicated new cellar door. "Everyone loved the barrel hall and we wanted to make it public," says estate winemaker and general manager Clare Halloran. "We wanted something different and looked to the wineries in France that are traditionally built underground for temperature control." She asserts, "There is a delightful element of surprise as you enter, not knowing what is behind the door. The beautiful and inviting underground space is what makes TarraWarra Estate unique."

Kerstin Thompson Architects (KTA) was appointed to design the new spaces, having impressed with their previous work on the estate in 1999. One of the challenges of the project was responding to the existing site conditions while creating a new environment that would both retain the original character and enhance the identity of TarraWarra Estate.

The architects presented their concept of a circular courtyard entrance, which incorporates stonework walls in keeping with the existing materials on the estate.

A local stonemason was employed to undertake the works, thereby meeting the environmental and localised remit.

The resultant cellar door provides a natural extension to the estate, which comprises a bar, lounge area and private dining room to create an intimate atmosphere within the Australian landscape, enriched by visual glimpses of surrounding vineyards. Internally, materials were chosen to complement the colour, taste and smell of the wines, while circular skylights filter sunlight down onto the polished concrete floor. "Its delight derives from combining an Australian landscape setting with the subterranean charm of a European wine cellar … while also creating a memorable experience for visitors, centred around wine and place," claims Kerstin Thompson.

In recognition of its unique and memorable design features, TarraWarra Estate became a worthy winner of a 2017 Australian Institute of Architects Victoria Chapter Commercial Chapter Award.

In addition to TarraWarra's aesthetic, wine-tasting and fine-dining attributes, visitors are guided through the winemaking process, from grape to glass, in line with the estate's educational principles. "For me it was about creating a welcoming and comfortable space. In the past there was not enough room for us to look after our customers properly. Now the long tasting bench encourages visitors to stay longer and we can engage with them more," Clare says.

When asked about feedback from visitors, Clare says all of it has been incredibly and overwhelmingly positive. "They are left with an impression that goes beyond a traditional wine-tasting visit, with the new subterranean cellar door helping the property secure its position as one of the most internationally lauded wineries in the Yarra Valley."

Yering Station
Yarra Valley

Embracing history

Located in the Yarra Valley wine region, Yering Station proudly boasts the oldest vineyard in Victoria, which was first planted back in 1838. The estate fully celebrates its past through the retention of the original avenue of elms, the heritage-listed barn and early winery building, which has been incorporated in the updated cellar door.

After changing hands several times during the early to mid-1990s, Yering Station was purchased by the Rathbone family in 1996. Their acclaimed winery subsequently garnered numerous prestigious honours, including International Winemaker of the Year at the 2004 International Wine and Spirit Competition, two years before the property itself was inducted into the Australian Tourism Awards Hall of Fame.

Most impressively perhaps, in 2015, Yering Station was declared one of 15 Architectural Masterpieces of the Wine World by Vivino, a London-based wine-tourism company, the only Australian winery to make the list.

Yering's wines are founded on the bridging point between old and new winemaking styles, and this respect for tradition was similarly prominent in the architectural concept design, inspired by a disused railway bridge in the historical local surrounds.

Owner, CEO and winemaker Darren Rathbone prepared the brief to create a winery designed for world-class, high-quality wine production.

As the site represented an existing attraction, the challenge for architect Robert Conti was to design a modern building that reflected the emergence of Australia as a premium wine-growing region, while acknowledging the original structures within the site. "The history of the site was a major attraction of the property, with an old timber-framed historic barn as well as the brick building that was the site of the initial winemaking facility and cellar-door sales," Robert says.

At the time, very few wineries in Australia provided food with wine tasting, so the architect and winery owners collaborated to expand the brief to fully encompass the notion of the winery as a standalone tourist destination, offering both wine and food experiences.

Yering had formed a partnership with a French Champagne house and expressed a desire for a traditional barrel cellar with vaulted and arched cellars such as those in European wineries. Robert proposed a location for the building on the side of a natural embankment that could be excavated to form concrete vaults, ideal for maintaining constant cellaring temperature and supporting the random flowing plan of the upper floor. "The excavation of the embankment also allowed us to minimise the visual presence of the building in order to accentuate the beauty of the natural environment," he recalls. Darren cites the underground barrel cellar as the stand-out part of the winery and believes the architect has created 'a very special, magical place'.

Robert recalls searching for contextual references in the region and how the elevated railway bridges created frames to the views beyond, forming the inspiration for the winery design. Yering Station's forecourt is defined by a long, curved wall constructed from locally sourced stone with its central opening framing the vineyards beyond. "The meandering wall, reflecting the backdrop of the mountain range, binds the various facilities and fragments at either end into a series of isolated stone columns that continue its presence infinitely into space," Robert says. "The central section is punctuated by a series of stone columns supporting a cantilevered skewed, stainless steel–clad canopy that frames the view of the landscape in a mannerism appropriating the railway trestle bridges."

The adjacent pedestrian path is the visual axis linking the historical barn, car park, winery and cellar-door building; a grassed forecourt forms a precinct of the winery buildings. Internally the circulation space allows for visibility throughout with this architectural element, providing the link between wine production and consumption. Careful planning of the layout allows visitors to participate in self-guided tours with viewpoints into every aspect of the winemaking process, from grape arrival, fermentation tanks, the cellaring of the wine and, finally, in-house tasting in the restaurant.

The combination of traditional and modern materials such as stone and metal symbolise the winemaking, which employs and respects age-old techniques enhanced by progressive style and sophistication. The stonework reflects the earth the vines grow in, the use of stainless steel alludes to the wine tanks, and the curved timber-lined roof in the restaurant give a sense of the inside of a wine barrel. Robert chose materials and forms found in the existing structures, thus establishing a silent dialogue between the key buildings. He also states the input of the winemaker in creating a footprint for the building design was very important, reinforcing the significance of the client-architect relationship. "An ambitious client with high expectations combined with an excellent builder results in high build quality," Robert notes.

Like a fine wine, the building has aged gracefully and timelessly and remains, more than 20 years after its construction, a major draw card for the property.

Summing up the fruition of his challenging brief, Darren says: "Creating a space that people feel comfortable in is important. It was very much about finding a balance, almost understated elegance. Overall, it is memorable without being overwhelming."

Yarra Valley 183

Jackalope Hotel
Mornington Peninsula

Redefining the wine destination

An astonishing Mornington Peninsula getaway, set on Willow Creek Vineyard in Merricks North, Jackalope Hotel is an absolute game changer that breaks all the rules to redefine the wine-destination experience. The brainchild of owner and entrepreneur Louis Li serenely combines the Edwardian homestead built in 1876 with a striking, ultra-modern 44-room hotel, an hour's drive from the Melbourne CBD.

The built form of Jackalope, named after a mythical North American creature, is hidden from the view of approaching visitors before its black sculptural form suddenly and dramatically appears. The siting of the main building pays implicit homage to Australian architectural typologies as an imposing agricultural barn structure and counterpoint to the existing winery. The building's black, metal-clad linear form with sawcut roof shapes nestles within the rugged landscape, providing a vivid visual contrast between the monolithic, seemingly anchored, structure and the rich green, red and silver foliage of adjacent vines.

In his brief for the development at Willow Creek Vineyard, Louis envisioned the hotel as "an exercise in conceiving the ultimate expression of regional luxury and exclusivity. It's about creating a sense of place. First and foremost, wine tasting is a sensory experience, so architecture offers a visual and tactile experience that complements the taste and smell of wine and food. Further, it's the first impressions, setting the scene of the experience that awaits."

Carr was appointed to undertake the design works in recognition of its previous success delivering imaginative projects that displayed great cultural awareness. Louis was delighted by the results, believing Carr's ability to achieve immersive storytelling far exceeded his original expectations.

Carr's response to the brief was "bold and adventurous in its design, guests are immersed in a journey that delights and surprises – successfully embracing its winemaking origins, yet celebrating a conceptual sensibility and sensory experience that is distinctive, magical and genuinely true to place".

The hotel story begins at arrival to Jackalope where a single-storey pavilion provides a contemporary link between the historical architecture of the restored heritage cottage and the imposing modernist new hotel. It acts as both connection and contrast between the two distinct building forms. Once inside, guests are immersed on a journey driven by the dynamic design of this new concept hotel. A dramatically lit black-glass box displaying wine stands as a monolithic object, underscoring the hotel's sense of purpose and place, setting the stage for the guest experience throughout the hotel.

The architect and interior designer describe the place as a celebration of 'alchemy and the art of transformation', while the spaces internally reflect and embrace the alchemist's workshop; eclectic, experimental and contemporary in detailing.

The signature bar is designed as the first stage of this guided alchemy concept, experimentation and transformation, sparking curiosity with its edgy and intriguing design as a taste of what is to follow. Located within the original nineteenth-century Federation cottage, the bar has been meticulously and sensitively restored, with interiors dominated by test-tube-like glass vessels lining the walls and a marble-clad bar acting as the alchemist's workbench.

The next stage in the alchemy process, discovery and intrigue, is represented by the stunning restaurant, where the spectacular light installation to the ceiling alludes to a dynamic and bubbling process.

One of many outstanding moments throughout the hotel, the 10,000 floating lights provide a clear reference to the conceptual design, transforming the space with a golden wave of light for the diners below.

Mornington Peninsula

Guest rooms have been designed with a sense of calm and sophistication, deliberately balancing the drama of the public spaces with tranquil individual retreats. The subtle and minimalist rooms are purposefully art-free, allowing the windows to frame the picturesque vineyard landscape beyond, accentuated by a shifting play of light and shadow as colours evolve with the time of day and seasons.

Distillation and transformation provide the concept for the hard and soft landscaping and public spaces, including a 30-metre (98-foot) infinity pool overlooking the vines.

A geode-like pavilion placed at the end of the pool deck serves as a multi-functional space to house intimate dining events and private wine tasting. The sharp edges and silver colours of its sculptural form enhance the wine immersion experience and provide yet another piece of drama so prevalent throughout the hotel.

Carr describes the whole design as "embracing the original concept of mystery and transformation, guiding guests through magical spaces".

A world-class collection of art, furniture and installations have been created specifically for the hotel, including the spectacular 7-metre (23-foot) *Jackalope* sculpture by local artist Emily Floyd. Its location at the entrance to the hotel alludes to the whimsical qualities of the hotel beyond.

The project has won countless architectural, interiors, and hospitality awards in the few years since opening. In 2017 it won an extraordinary trio of awards from *Gourmet Traveller Australia Hotel Guide* – Hotel, New Hotel and Regional Hotel of the Year.

Every detail has been thoughtfully considered at Jackalope, resulting in a sensory experience that is truly distinctive and unique, and the ultimate escape from reality.

Montalto
Mornington Peninsula

Worth the wait

Montalto is a testament to the virtues of patience and determination, given the long gestation period before owners John and Wendy Mitchell realised their dream, first formed in the 1980s when they lived in the UK and summered among the vineyards in the south of France.

Upon their return to Australia in 1990, the couple planted a few vines at their house on the Mornington Peninsula coast as John set about learning his chosen craft by studying viticulture at the University of Melbourne's Dookie campus. After researching coastal vineyards, they eventually purchased land in the heart of Red Hill South, a 70-minute drive south of Melbourne CBD, at the site that was to become the family-owned and run Montalto Estate, which opened to the public in January 2002.

Along with a group of close friends including architect Peter Williams, whom he had known for years and regularly made clear his winery-owning intentions, John embarked on a collaborative journey discussing and proposing how the property he had purchased could be developed. There was a continuous exploration of ideas and values, and the consensus was to 'bring the outside in' and allow visitors to focus on the external environments, almost imagining the building disappear within the landscape.

Peter's Melbourne-based architectural practice, Williams Boag Architects, was engaged to plan and design the structures, comprising a restaurant, cellar door, storage and amenity facilities. "Our philosophy was to introduce buildings onto the site that not only preserved the qualities of the surrounding landscape but celebrated it and 'introduced' visitors to it," Peter recalls.

The site was developed as a venue for visitors to the Mornington Peninsula and the local community to enjoy the regional produce, hospitality and beauty found in the extensive natural systems on and around the site. John admits that people like himself and his friends were the target market and they were keen to share the authenticity of their project.

The winery draws strongly on the undulation of the sloping grounds and employs four main architectural elements: a raised earth berm, a core structure, a concealed

courtyard and a landscape frame element. The response to the ambience of the setting is non-obtrusive and the winery architecture nurtures the landscape.

Raw materials are used throughout, including rammed-earth walls and exposed concrete floors that have been polished over time by people's feet. John loves the cantilever deck at the front of the restaurant, where the laminated beams express the connection between the building and the landscape.

The spaces create a variety of experiences for the wine-tasting public, including a warm and welcoming cellar door, an exclusive wine room, a hatted restaurant, and a piazza that allows guests to drink in the breathtaking views of the estate.

Montalto, which prides itself on offering a 'moment out of the ordinary', incorporates a sculptural trail of more than 30 permanent sculptures sensitively sited throughout the grounds, ranging from huge works in open spaces to more intimate pieces among the wetlands and vines.

The winery hosts many events throughout the year that use this series of spaces, which also frame the panoramic views to the wetlands and beyond. Ultimately, they have built a place for visitors to enjoy. The grounds offer peaceful and beautiful walks through the olive trees, boardwalks through the wetlands, extensive kitchen gardens, and the award-winning restaurant, which has become well known as a highlight at the estate.

The contemporary and thoughtfully considered architectural and landscape design has resulted in a timeless elegance and it is surprising to learn that the building is almost 20 years old. John recalls their original design vision was for a beautiful aged quality and believes that as an early player in the region, Montalto has helped to redefine the visitor experience to the Mornington Peninsula.

As a testament to its success, Montalto has received a Merit Award from the Australian Institute of Architects Awards for Commercial Architecture in 2002, Best Winery Tourism Destination by *Gourmet Traveller* magazine, and a five-star rating by Australian wine critic and vigneron James Halliday.

"There is absolutely no doubt that the architecture enhances the wine-tasting experience, and the buildings are immediately connected with the wine landscape," John says.

Peter concurs, noting: "The project nurtures the wine landscape and prevailing natural systems, promoting an exemplary active and responsible management of the site to be enjoyed now and into the future."

Mornington Peninsula

Polperro
Mornington Peninsula

Passion project

Vintner and owner Sam Coverdale established Polperro by Even Keel in 2006, following a diverse geographical winemaking career that encompassed legendary grape-growing regions across Australia, France, Italy and Spain.

Raised in northern New South Wales and south-east Queensland, a business and wines science graduate who began work as a vintage cellar hand at 18 years old, Sam set up Polperro with the intention of creating drinkable, balanced and elegant wines that continue to interest beyond the first glass.

The Polperro location perfectly reflects his professional and personal passions, with its vineyards, nearby surf beaches and close proximity to Melbourne making Mornington Peninsula the ideal home for Sam and his family.

Sam's winemaking philosophy plays to strengths of the region by being true to the climatic conditions of each vintage, while individual vineyard characters employ a mix of traditional and modern practices that ensure minimal intervention and sustainability.

To complement his winemaking vision, the construction of a new cellar door with restaurant and accommodation villas was planned, to offer visitors and guests the opportunity to immerse themselves in an authentic vineyard, food and wine experience. Hecker Guthrie were approached in 2013 to redesign the interiors of the existing buildings and create something unique on the Peninsula at an amazing site – a mix of old and new, rustic but warm, homely and familiar.

"We have found from previous experience, that wine people are inherently passionate people. Passionate and enthusiastic clients make for an engaged and enjoyable design process which in turn leads to successful design outcomes," recalls Hamish Guthrie, director at Hecker Guthrie. "The space was to encompass a feeling of passion and represent the level of craft required to cultivate and produce such wine. Incorporating a sense of artisan or craft in the detailing of each element."

Hamish and his team have achieved this by creating an environment with a colour palette naturally derived from the immediate landscape, but with an urban approach. Through design, the winery can become a three-dimensional embodiment of the wine brand. Hamish believes the role of designers is to assist the client in achieving

"a recognisable embodiment of their passion and commitment to the location, the food and wine offering, and the experience." While the interior becomes the recognisable face of the winery, it is the experiences here and the mood it evokes that are key to the success of Polperro.

When asked how does he think the design enhances the winery experience, Hamish responds, "The understated approach to the design is there to create the environment around which the wine and food are elevated and the experiences around their enjoyment is celebrated."

The designers knew the vineyard view is key to the success of any winery, but at Polperro they wanted to provide an intimate connection with touchpoints to other parts of the room too, so "there are no bad tables at the restaurant."

Boutique accommodation on the working property includes four beautifully styled luxury villas and a farmhouse that evokes the iconic Australian 1950s holiday home. There is a focus on social living and connection to the outside; both the vineyard and distant ocean views provide a backdrop to spaces that have been created for retreat and relaxation. Polperro was awarded the Most Relaxing Vineyard Stay at the LUX International Hotel and Spa Awards, and the latest addition to the winery experience is the HotHut, is a small boutique yoga studio, which maximises the benefits of its natural surrounds.

In identifying what makes Polperro stand out from the many other wineries in the region, Hamish cites a very strong sense of place in the way it connects interior with the landscape and vineyards. "The point of difference here is it sensitively reflects the personalities of its owners and makers. There is an intimate, relaxed and understated approach to the design here. Almost effortless, which conceals the curated and crafted approach."

Port Phillip Estate
Mornington Peninsula

An alchemy of architecture and wine

What began as a modest retirement project subsequently evolved into one of the shining jewels of the Mornington Peninsula wine region, with panoramic views over undulating vineyards and the sea.

Following the initial acquisition of the Port Phillip Estate vineyard in 2000, Giorgio Gjergja, a successful electrical manufacturer, and wife Dianne grew the operations exponentially before passing over the reins to children Marco and Melissa 10 years later.

"Originally it started as a hobby business with just 4 hectares (10 acres) under vines and where we just grew the fruit. These days we have about 60 hectares (150 acres), a cellar door, restaurant and accommodation," Marco says.

The purchase of Kooyong winery and vineyards in 2004 underscored the scale of the family's ambitions and led, naturally, to the construction of a single, unifying cellar door where over 20 estate and single-vineyard wines can be sampled. "We found this parcel of land and the business owner was keen to sell it so we knew this was the perfect location for our restaurant and cellar door. Mum always had a keen interest in architecture so we started sourcing architects together," says Marco.

According to Marco, the design vision was to "deliver the unexpected where the natural meets contemporary design." They wanted to produce something that couldn't already be imagined; uncompromising architecture.

Marco had long admired the Australian Centre for Contemporary Art in Melbourne's Southbank arts precinct, designed by Wood Marsh Architects. He improvised a tour of other projects by the architects, and when the tour was over the family decided to commission Wood Marsh. "We loved the work of Roger Wood and Randall Marsh and their very solid brutalist sculpture style and wanted something that we couldn't dream up ourselves," Marco and Melissa recall.

The architects responded to the brief with a sensitivity to the environment and provided a robust building that celebrates the rural seaside landscape and maritime context. According to Wood Marsh: "It encapsulates the essence of winemaking and presents a bold and simple gesture to the public."

"When the plans were revealed, it was not what we had expected. We had seen very rectangular shapes with these architects and this was quite different. It turned out to be even better than we expected," says Marco.

Port Phillip Estate emanates from the landscape as it unfurls across the ridge, spiralling from the ground and rising to form the dramatic 120-metre-long (394-foot-long) wall. This abstract sculptural form made from limestone rammed earth conceals much of the building.

Roger Wood, founding partner of Wood Marsh, describes the organic form of the building: "Understanding the importance of temperature stability in winemaking and looking at the site, we thought it would be a great idea to bury a substantial portion of the building. The submerged oval shape spirals out of the ground as an earth wall with a single portal entry, simultaneously creating a barrier to the view upon approach. The form is meant to look like a relic from an ancient civilisation, like an Inca ruin built long ago, and through erosion, it's been exposed over time. Similarly, it could have been a giant fossil of a whale or a massive broken shell that has washed up in a from the Jurassic period."

Overlooking picturesque vineyards, Westernport Bay and Bass Strait, the heavy wall is punctured by the main entry, which reveals a striking vista to the coastal views beyond. A large restaurant and cellar door with an outdoor terrace also take full advantage of this view.

A grand ceremonial staircase leads down past the administration areas into the underbelly of the building where state-of-the-art bottling facilities are housed. The ceiling of the barrel storage room is reminiscent of a cathedral undercroft, and a deliberate layering of functionality to the building includes luxury accommodation below the restaurant.

Roger recalls, "We based the submerged cellar on an abstraction of a sixteenth-century French wine château. In the Bordeaux and Burgundy regions, the wineries would have chalk caves underground, and production, offices and accommodation on separate levels above. Combining those ideas with the environmental considerations, the wine storage and barrel room is buried to maintain consistent temperature and humidity, which is critical in winemaking. As in the château model, the stair becomes the conduit between the chalk cave and the accommodation. We wanted it to be a grand and powerful statement because it links the function of the building to the enjoyment of the building – the winemaking and the wine drinking."

The architects have used a restrained palette of materials throughout the building 'referencing textures and colours that are reminiscent of the harsh Australian environment'. Burnt timbers and sun-bleached rammed earth feature predominantly, highlighting their inherent character.

The practical nature of the building includes many sustainable features, reflective of the ongoing philosophy of environmental responsibility at Wood Marsh, and a fundamental tenet of all the Gjergja family businesses. The exterior walls shield interior spaces from the low sun and provide excellent insulation while the below-ground barrel room forms a natural temperature-controlled cellar space, without the need for air-conditioning.

Port Phillip Estate was honoured with two prestigious awards at the 2010 Australian Institute of Architects Awards – the National Award for Commercial Architecture and the National Award for Interior Architecture, as well as top prize for Commercial Architecture at the 2010 Victorian Architecture Awards. The jury concluded, "The architectural quality, the quality of the wine, food and hospitality merge completely to form one immensely satisfying experience."

The importance of the architecture in enhancing this wine destination is conveyed with the prominent placement of the architectural model in the main entrance foyer of the estate, where visitors cannot help but stop and admire the beautiful curved conceptual forms.

Roger believes, "By investing in architecture, our client showed enormous confidence in the wine industry and specifically the Mornington Peninsula region." An investment that has clearly paid off.

Pt Leo Estate
Mornington Peninsula

Wine and sculpture

Exceptional even among the collection of new and exciting venues on the picturesque Mornington Peninsula, Pt Leo Estate has evolved into an internationally renowned, multi-faceted winery destination. Exquisitely perched on the edge of pristine Melbourne coastline, Pt Leo has come a long way since the Gandel family planted their first vineyard on part of a massive farmland property formerly owned by the Cole family from Federation to the late 1960s. Having collected over 50 significant large-scale sculptures over their lifetime, the owners envisioned opening their collection to the public, alongside the launch of their first wine label.

Jolson Architecture & Interior Design were invited to prepare concept designs for their new estate comprising a cellar door and restaurants. "The brief was unique and brings together art, wine, food and architecture within a building, located within a sculpture park," recalls owner and director Stephen Jolson, whose team responded with an architectural concept that was about "how to enhance the vineyard experience."

Set on the highest point of the (20-hectare) 50-acre estate and offering sweeping views out to the ocean, Pt Leo Estate opened in 2017 and celebrates a sense of place, and offers an unforgettable wine experience. A grand curved forecourt provides visitors with a stunning sculptural welcome, and a single 70-year old bottle tree marks the entrance; the doorway beyond offers a glimpse of the building within.

Jolson describe the architecture as being "deeply embedded in context, the building rises from the ground as an abstract architectural gesture following the curving nature of the site, referencing the process of winemaking and taking on a subtle sculptural quality of its own. The curvaceous form is an abstract interpretation of wine pouring from a bottle and the organic cycle of the wine harvest. Internally, the building takes inspiration from a deconstructed wine barrel, with a predominance of steel and timber lining the surfaces."

It was important that sight lines were deliberately created and maintained between the internal spaces and external surroundings, providing connections to the vines and sculptures. "The building has an intentional humility when viewed from within the sculpture park. Its presence diminishes with the radial sweep of the building emphasising the art itself."

The imaginative placement of sculptures throughout the landscaping and vineyards creates a unique, standalone contemporary art display that guests can enjoy, alongside their fine food and wine tasting adventures. Hassell Studio designed the landscape for the sculpture park, which allows visitors to experience the significant collection up close and personally. The outdoor gallery in set within 125 hectares (309 acres) of landscaped grounds, with both a gentle promenade and strenuous trek provided to view the large-scale works.

Jaume Plensa, George Rockey, Tony Cragg, Inge King, Lenton Parr and KAWS are among the artists on display in the park, which remains a work in progress for future acquisitions and commissions.

As a destination, "Pt Leo is a sculptural gesture externally, but the instant you move through the entrance your focus shifts to the other elements of the building and the stunning rugged Australian landscape. In this instance, the architecture has its distinct contribution to the physical nature of where these aspects come together, but it is also a part of creating a richer interaction between each," according to the Jolson team.

Discerning foodies are drawn to Laura, an intimate and exclusive two-hatted restaurant set within the grounds, and Pt Leo Restaurant with its modern space and open kitchen overlooking the sculpture park through to the views beyond.

Careful attention to the distinctive Australian menu, and care provided by the Pt Leo staff ensure a high number of return visitors – a clear testament to its success.

Countless awards have been earned including the *Good Food Guide*, Australian Wine List of the Year, and the Victorian Landscape Architecture Awards.

The experience of this destination is not only about the architecture or the art, or the vines. It is the synthesis of all of these things, together with its context, that makes it resonate.

Ten Minutes by Tractor
Mornington Peninsula

Rising from the ashes

The intriguing and evocatively named Ten Minutes by Tractor is located at the convergence of a trio of vineyards in the central hinterland of the Mornington Peninsula district of Main Ridge.

These three family-owned vineyards, each located a 10-minute tractor ride from the others, began almost 30 years ago and have been added to since the winery started in 1997, producing wines with their own distinct quality and character that can seem worlds apart.

Current owner Martin Spedding came across Ten Minutes by Tractor during his search through Victoria, Tasmania and New Zealand for a winery that offered great potential, a place where he could work and live for the rest of his life. After a visit to the cellar door and discovering that the families were looking for someone to take over their winery, Martin immediately knew it was the place he had been looking for and embarked upon "the beginning of an exciting new adventure and a jumble of hopes and dreams about the future."

His aspirations for the winery, whose original cellar door was set in an old tin shed that previously served as horses stables, were continual improvement, determined by his dedication to learning about producing outstanding wines and the places that define them.

"The plan was to try and find a permanent home for Ten Minutes by Tractor, a place where we could welcome visitors, work and bring together all the elements of our winery to be able to showcase our wines, and tell our story," Martin says.

Martin and his wife Karen soon located a nearby site – almost perfectly aligned between their three vineyards – that was ideal for relocating the cellar door and building a restaurant. It needed a lot of work and Martin set about developing plans "with a focus on how we could extend our wine-tasting experience to encompass food and wine matching and showcase the local produce of the Mornington Peninsula." After opening in late 2006, the restaurant received an abundance of awards and accolades as it established a reputation as the best restaurant in the region.

The Speddings' dream was subsequently shattered when a huge fire at the start of 2018 forced them to close the venue having lost almost everything, including

16,000 bottles of wine and vineyard equipment. "We watched as the inferno took hold of the old shed and watched it burn to the ground," Martin recounts. "It was a devastating day. The loss of so much of what we had built over the previous 15 years. Once the urgency of our business survival and the relocation of our cellar door and business to another site had passed, we started the slow process of planning and designing a new home for our winery."

Their vision was to build a new building to replace what had been lost in the fire; to house a new cellar door, tasting rooms, a wine gallery, offices and newly imagined restaurant within a fully integrated site incorporating the innovative working vineyard.

Martin was determined to retain the character and integrity of the original cottage while creating a clear and strong relationship to the new build that was visually seamless and authentic. Close friend Patrick Ness, director at one of Australia's leading architectural practices, Cox Architecture, took on the unique regional project, partly due to his personal connection.

"The relationship between the client and the architect is critical to the success of any project. The ability to synthesise ideas, work closely and collaboratively on what, in the end, is a shared vision and design," Martin says. "Patrick, Karen and I had a strong connection and alignment around the design principles, the aesthetic direction and on how best to work together. Patrick and his team quickly embraced the brief and generated some great design concepts on how to achieve our objectives and to incorporate our ideas into their design. It was a great partnership."

Patrick considered the whole design as an events platform "in which every element (dining, tasting, winemaking, viewing, working, learning) had places to support

these activities. Multiple settings all provide varied and purposeful places for human endeavour."

The entrance to the cellar door, in particular, is quite spectacular. There is a polished stone cement floor, a tasting bench designed to depict the different vineyard soil profiles, and a simple glazed window connecting wine tasters to the elements that contribute to the contents of their wine glass. When the visitor looks up, however, they cannot help but be amazed by the incredible and stunning vaulted timber baton ceiling that leads to the skylight – Martin's favourite place in the winery. "It provides a great sense of space and purpose and connects with you in a very convincing way. It is unexpected and I think gives visitors a great rush of excitement when they enter the room, and great anticipation of what is to follow," Martin notes.

Patrick surmises, "At first glance there is a reserved and utilitarian nature to the architecture. A simple shed with some additions to the restaurant. Deliberately understated and only doing what was needed. Volumes, areas and functionality just enough to do what was required. And then moments of unexpected delight in places like the cellar door, glimpses of the vineyard between buildings. A pragmatic and poetic approach that does not overwhelm the act of hospitality or the skill and intent of the winemaking itself."

Explaining what makes Ten Minutes by Tractor stand out among the 200 vineyards, 60 wineries and at least 50 cellar doors on the Mornington Peninsula, Martin claims, "The architecture has successfully created spaces and connections that elevate the whole wine-tasting experience and provides a stage on which we can showcase our wines, tell our stories and add further dimensions and depth to a visit."

Mitchelton
Nagambie

Towering history

Named in honour of explorer Major Thomas Mitchell, who came across the Goulburn Valley site during an historic 900-kilometre (560-mile) Melbourne to Sydney trek in 1836, Mitchelton Estate was established over a century later by entrepreneur Ross Shelmerdine. Shortly after Ross planted the first crops in 1969, designs for a winery and cellar door were entrusted to one of Australia's most renowned architects, Robin Boyd CBE.

Robin's vision, including the astonishing 55-metre (180-foot) tower, became a reality in 1974 under the direction of acclaimed architect successor Ted Ashton, who took over the project's reins following Robin's untimely death three years earlier.

Rows of nurtured vineyards welcome visitors along a driveway on their approach to the tower, which has become a recognised icon of the Victorian winemaking landscape and features proudly on several Mitchelton wine labels.

Father-and-son owners, Gerry and Andrew Ryan, grabbed an opportunity to purchase the property in 2011 and set about revitalising the award-winning winery while maintaining a connection to its strong history and unique architecture. The re-development brief was in two parts; initially the cellar door, restaurant and function space refurbishments, followed by a new luxury boutique hotel, which opened in 2018.

"We wanted to respect the architecture of Robin Boyd so we focused on the joinery, soft furnishings and landscaping rather than the architecture. It was about respect for what was already there," Andrew explains. "The hotel has always been the missing piece in the puzzle for Mitchelton and it was important that it fitted into the architectural landscape and complement it rather than to take over and be the hero."

The winery's partnership with leading architects continued with the engagement in 2012 of Hecker Guthrie to design a new cellar door and 58-room hotel. Andrew knew they were the right fit for the project and would "work with the initial architecture rather than try to change it."

Hamish Guthrie recalls the key design requirements were to "borrow from the existing modern lines, rustic textures and sculptural forms." Their response was a concept that would reflect the rich history of Mitchelton that was authentic and refined.

Nagambie

In considering how the design contributes to establishing the winery as a destination and enhancing the wine-tasting experience, Andrew believes it is "terribly important, if done correctly."

Hamish understood they were working with a very significant building that needed to be approached and considered appropriately. "The architecture is on a large scale; it is strong, rigorous and grounded. We wanted to be sensitive to the architectural heritage whilst updated to the demands of a contemporary working winery in the hands of a new owner." Hecker Guthrie decided a limited palette of natural materials was the right approach to take for a building immersed in a beautiful vineyard in the middle of the country.

Another design decision was for all joinery to be made on-site by the builder, due to the remoteness of the site location. "This not only informed our approach to the design of the fixtures but has bought a beautiful raw and handmade quality to these items," Hamish states.

The sense of scale and space when walking through the property is also heightened by the awareness of the underground cellar, which is currently the largest operating cellar in the southern hemisphere, differentiating the winery from most in the world. "Given the vastness of the existing architecture, our intention was to bring the focus to a more intimate relationship with the product (the wine) and to celebrate the experience around the product. The interior elevates the wine, while the materiality and the fixtures bring the experience back to a human scale," Hecker Guthrie declares. "The unique aspect of this will always remain the significant architectural pedigree and heritage. And its scale!"

In addition to the immense cellar, the estate features The Mitchelton Gallery of Aboriginal Art, the largest Indigenous art gallery in regional Victoria. The permanent exhibition displays works created by some of Australia's most revered Indigenous artists, and the Gallery Director is the President of the Aboriginal Art Association of Australia. The space provides yet another layer of inspiring experiences for locals and visitors at Mitchelton.

Ashton Tower remains the standout feature of the winery, with Andrew particularly enjoying how the sun lights up its different sides, especially towards the end of the day when the sun is setting.

The Mitchelton wine destination experience is aptly summarised by the estate motto: "Look for the Tower. We'll open the wine."

Leura Park
Bellarine Peninsula

Attention grabbing design

A boutique estate set on Victoria's Bellarine Peninsula, Leura Park enjoys a well-earned reputation as an exceptional producer of premium, cool maritime climate wines, ideally sampled from its rustic, curvaceous cellar door.

Established by David and Lyndsay Sharp in 1995, the estate includes 16 hectares (40 acres) of vineyards where hand-picked grapes are delivered to acclaimed winemaker Darren Burke, who employs *méthode traditionelle* to create distinctive and delightful wines, encapsulating French-style subtlety.

While distinctive and delightful fit equally well as adjectives for the new Leura Park winery pavilion, subtlety is not a description that springs to mind for a building named 'The Vault', following a naming competition upon its completion. The Vault certainly achieves the owners' request for a stand-out building that provides a visual point of difference for the region and not 'just another winery shed'. Lyndsay recalls her brief to the architects was a simple, "Give me a shed with a hair-do," which reflects Leura Park Estate's "friendly, artisan soul."

Centrum Architects were an easy choice to undertake the design, further to their work on Leura Park's other venue builds including Jack Rabbit Vineyard Restaurant and Flying Brick Cider House. "We have always worked really well with Centrum – they listen and will always take on board our vision for both aesthetic and functional patron service-focused perspective," Lyndsay says.

In 2012 the architects set about designing the new pavilion that would replace an existing temporary tent shelter that had become a permanent installation.

Andrew Rowe, design director at Centrum Architects, recalls that in addition to the unusual initial brief from Lyndsay, "The Leura Park Winery pavilion needed to attract people – an attention-grabbing highway lantern luring patrons to enter, taste, eat and enjoy."

From the architects' point of view, the creative challenge was meeting the client's expectations in an authentic manner and with a meaningful endurance. Andrew wanted to ensure they delivered "something to outlast a fashionable hair-do." "At Centrum we believe true architecture embodies the union of people and place, inspired by a unique story – making places that connect people to their world and enriching lives," Andrew says. "We love creating architecture that transcends pure function and we need to connect people with their environment(s) – a unique combination of built, social, historical and natural."

Drawing inspiration from the word 'Leura', which is derived from the Aboriginal word meaning 'lava', Centrum researched images of lava flows cooling and solidifying, and incorporated these ideas into the structural concrete forms. The shells rise out of the ground and fold over, shunning the wind and western sun to shelter and embrace the grassed forecourt, and at night the pavilion is evocative of a roadside lantern. In terms of construction, the geometry of each roof and wall shell was standardised to suit precast concrete panels.

The resulting venue is unmissable and attracts a lot of attention. The owners claim it is often referred to as 'The Opera House of the Bellarine' and since completion opinions have been polarising. "Most people love it but there are a handful who think it's hideous!"

The curved concrete forms of 'The Vault' are certainly a subject of discussion by guests, and the large glazed fire-station doors open out to the external grassed area, facilitating an indoor–outdoor aesthetic and functionality. Porthole windows are randomly dotted across the backdrop of concrete waves, providing further connection to the outside.

Wine experiences on offer at Leura Park Estate are enhanced by the space, particularly the intimate 'Paint & Sip' classes and interactive cooking classes.

Lyndsay believes the architecture "cocoons people in a unique, friendly contemporary space, and it's very rare for people to not be smiling when they are inside The Vault. The whole vibe is enchanting. You can't help but walk inside and feel both inspired and happy."

As for Andrew, he suggests Leura Park "has a vibe that echoes Lyndsay's character – fun, energetic, but also laid-back and eclectic. The pavilion has become a stage for that sort of life." "Beyond the pragmatic needs, our 'shed with a hair-do' has succeeded by attracting people, causing drivers to swing into the car park and check it out during the quiet weekdays and stop for pizza and a drink on the weekend," he says.

The Vault has become an unexpected icon for Bellarine Peninsula tourism, and people are encouraged to engage with the architecture, hang out, relax and enjoy life.

As Andrew aptly puts it: "The Vault is the backdrop – the blank canvas for all the colour of life."

Clover Hill
Piper's River

Royal sparkle

Makers of some of Australia's finest sparkling-wine, named after its rolling hills and lush golden Tasmanian clover, Clover Hill has proven itself a worthy rival of the great Champagne houses of France.

Concluding an exhaustive search for an ideal location with the sole purpose of producing traditionally made, world-class sparkling wine, Clover Hill was founded in 1986 by the Goelet family on the site of a small former dairy farm surrounded by natural forest.

The first vintage five years later turned the owners' pioneering vision into a reality, laying down the foundation for the flavour and structure core of its elegant wines that have helped secure Clover Hill a reputation for its distinguished Tasmanian style and intriguing royal patronage.

Clover Hill was served at Princess Mary and Crown Prince Frederick's royal wedding celebrations in Denmark in 2004, and then selected as one of the four iconic Australian wines for Queen Elizabeth II and the Duke of Edinburgh during their 2011 visit to Australia.

Underlining the commitment to its original concept to produce sophisticated sparkling wine, the traditional 'Trinity' varietals of Chardonnay, Pinot Noir and Pinot Meunier are symbolised in the three-leaf-clover design of the Clover Hill wine brand. Equally symbolic, the cellar door opened in 2017 has a striking design based on the shape of a clover leaf – positioned at the top of the valley overlooking the surrounding vineyard, forests and Bass Straight.

Adam Torpy, CEO of Clover Hill, who brought 20 years of international wine-industry experience when he joined the estate in 2005, was involved in all aspects of the building process from the initial brief requirements to project completion. His philosophy in winemaking is for greatness, appreciation and enjoyment – attributes that can also be applied to his approach to the cellar-door design. Adam believes the land characteristics are an integral component of great wine, and this is embodied in his view on how the architecture contributes to the winery as a destination. "There's a huge movement in the Australian industry at the moment with regard to landscape integration and impactful designs that reflect a winery's uniqueness, and I can safely

say you'll see no other cellar door like this," says Adam. "It's wonderful to think that everything we do at Clover Hill comes from this land and that the cellar door might give us another way to educate wine lovers about what makes the Lebrina site special."

David Gillies, architect and director at 6ty degrees, who was engaged to undertake the design stages, recalls how the resolution of the building reflects the place. "The new cellar door takes up a commanding position over the vines; they fall away beneath it towards the low-lying bush in the valley below. On those perfect spring northern Tasmanian days, the distant waters of Bass Strait offer an end note for the distant gaze before the focus returns once again to the cellar door."

The brief requirements were to capture this outlook, and the building form was defined by a geometric axis that formed connections to the landscape. Intersecting walls rise from the ground, while the tasting room and external deck are located in the quadrant boasting the panoramic views.

The carefully considered selection of materials is a key feature of the design, with a focus on earthy tones and natural elements, reinforcing the relationship to the setting. In addition to rammed-earth walls, Corten cladding and native timbers have been used in the construction. "The stunning surroundings captivate visitors, the cellar door had to draw attention back to itself. Using materials, texture, colour and detail, it was designed to complement rather than challenge its setting and subtly draw people into its embrace," notes David. "The architecture requests people to stop, look and think about the Clover Hill experience as they walk beside the rammed-earth wall that leads them into the main tasting room and out into the vineyard beyond."

Adam envisioned, "landscape integration and impactful architectural design" and utilising materials that would create "a modern building that was created to grow old." Since the build completion, the Clover Hill cellar door has received national recognition for its unique architecture, contributing to an exceptional experience for all visitors. The natural integration with the Tasmanian landscape enables visitors to feel connected to the terroir of the vineyard and the creation of the wines.

"We've created nooks throughout the cellar-door space in an effort to foster a laid-back atmosphere, where from every point your eye is led down into the vines – where we encourage visitors to take a wander and enjoy all that Clover Hill has to offer," says Adam, who identifies the walk through the front entrance as his favourite part of Clover Hill. "We have a mysterious entry where you're not sure what is there and, once inside, there's a view from every aspect. You can see Bass Strait on a good day, with a 100-metre (328-foot) drop to the bottom of the vineyard."

Clover Hill cellar door sets itself apart though its extremely modern building and commitment to offering premium, luxurious natural surroundings in which to relax and taste the world-class sparkling wines.

Devil's Corner
Apslawn

A lookout for wine

Reminiscent of cargo boxes lost at sea, Devil's Corner is a beautiful juxtaposition of forms perched on land that delivers a daring destination for architecture and wine lovers alike. Named after nearby rugged waters, the dramatic meeting of vines and rolling waves off the east coast of Tasmania, Devil's Corner provides an exciting backdrop for both vintner and architect to demonstrate their adventurous spirits.

Brown Brothers, having acquired the vineyard site in 2010, set about creating a new tourism experience with the construction of a safe outlook at one of the largest vineyards in the area, which amplified an existing iconic view of the Hazards Range. "We wanted a home for our Devil's Corner Tasmania brand that was located on the vineyard where the grapes are grown. We also wanted to share the amazing location with visitors; local, interstate and international," explains Will Adkins of the Brown Family Wine Group. They envisioned a series of buildings that settled into the landscape, put people at ease and were tactile. "We wanted a place that people came to meet, enjoy our wines and some local food," as Will puts it.

Because of the site's wild nature and challenging elements, easy-build structures were required for the remote location. They did not expect polished finishes throughout but rather a place that reflected the values of a wine brand that was accessible to visitors.

Renowned for its extraordinary, ambitious projects and led by a commitment to enduring and functional design, Cumulus Studio was engaged to help define the concept and realise the client's vision, which was unveiled to the public in December 2015. "Cumulus is well known in Tasmania, having done some great work in remote and wild locations, and understood the style and feel of the site and buildings that we sought," Will remembers.

They were appointed to extend and expand the original small demountable building – a veritable tin shed – in addition to creating a dynamic, memorable observation tower and associated facilities that would draw visitors to the Devil's Corner wine label.

The cellar door and lookout were designed as a loose collection of timber-clad buildings that, through similar aesthetic and material treatment, form a modern interpretation of a traditional rural settlement over time. The building forms are

collected around a courtyard space allowing shelter and respite from the surrounding environment, while providing views through the tasting space and access to the open deck.

Thanks to the careful placement of a series of shipping container, visitors are invited to visually explore the landscape within and around the vineyard through curated framed views. The integral strength of the containers made them an ideal choice in the construction of the lookout in particular, by enabling the structure of the building to be delivered to the site and erected quickly. Each container has been modified in various ways – the cranked 'sky' lookout cut from two parts of a single unit and reassembled; the 'horizon' lookout, which is able to bridge the land and the 'tower' despite one side being cut out; and the 'tower' lookout constructed from two containers end-on-end. Inside the latter, steel-plate stairs wind up past projecting landings on each side. These landings provide views over the landscape as the viewer moves up the tower; the black-steel box frames fixed to the container cantilever over the vineyard.

This design concept purposefully focuses the viewing areas into three curated frames, an idea inspired by wine, according to architect Peter Walker. "When tasting wine, we are encouraged to be aware of various aspects of the wine and associated taste sensations," Peter says. "By providing a variety of distinct, unique ways in which visitors to the site can experience and understand the surrounding landscape, we intended to subtly reference the experience of wine tasting."

The lookout element is a critical component of the design, providing a visual signifier for the settlement that pulls in people off the road and as a way of interpreting the landscape from which the Devil's Corner wines originate.

It was important to Cumulus Studio that the cellar door felt like it was sitting in the vineyard and connected to the place where the wines originate. "The tower was envisioned as not only a prominent signpost for the project that would attract visitors into the site, but also as a unique tourism experience that people would share," declares Peter.

The architectural award–winning cellar door and lookout allow guests to enjoy the scenic view while tasting wine and sampling fresh seafood from a local oyster farmer at The Fishers, or pizza and gelato at Tombolo.

Local markets and seasonal events are held throughout the year at Devil's Corner, which combines dramatic location, view, buildings and vineyard to offer significantly more than a standard wine-tasting venue.

Apslawn

Moorilla at MONA
Hobart

State of the art

The second oldest winery in Tasmania, Moorilla, which means 'rock by the water' according to various Aboriginal dialects, was established in 1962 on property purchased 14 years earlier by famed Italian-Australian industrialist and patron of the arts, Claudio Alcorso.

The land's winemaking potential may have been recognised as far back as 1798, when George Bass sailed past with Matthew Flinders and allegedly remarked that its stiff close soil was "perhaps adapted to the growth of grape vines, rather than of grain."

Claudio, the creator of premium Australian textile Sheridan, commissioned legendary architect Roy Grounds to design modernist dwellings on the site for his family, and planted the first vine cuttings.

Admiring Moorilla's architecture from his home across the river, David Walsh purchased the winery in 1995 'on a whim', initially as a site for an art warehouse before he became enamoured by the art of winemaking.

A decade later, a pub discussion between David and Craig Rosevear of Rosevear Stephenson architects heralded the next stage in Moorilla's wine and design progression – the construction of a new wine-tasting bar and restaurant to be named The Ether Building.

Craig says the main purpose of the new building was "to provide a new front face of an established business proud of its quality and integrity, the building is unapologetic but restrained in character. The architecture seeks to engage with, but not diminish these existing qualities."

To ensure the building reflected its context, Craig says the intention was "to capitalise on sun and views of the river and the wider landscape and to provide a strong public face to the estate, and sited immediately adjacent to the outdoor winemaking facility so that patrons can watch the winery at work."

Rosevear Stephenson worked in association with JAWS Architects to design and deliver the modern building which received both an Australian Institute of Architects Awards Tasmania Commercial Award and National Commendation in 2006.

"Buying Moorilla was one of the best decisions I've ever made," declares David, who convinced winemaker Conor van der Reest to join him to redefine the estate and help design a new state-of-the-art winery in 2007. Having spent years gaining experience in old and new winemaking techniques around the globe, Conor was given free reign at Moorilla, where he has proven himself by producing leading wines in the region.

Fender Katsalidis was engaged to design the Museum of Old and New Art (MONA) within the Moorilla Estate, and the first step was to create a masterplan for the site that determined how to place the gallery and relocate the existing winery.

"Moorilla has a long history, by Tasmanian winery standards, and we attempted to make that history readable on the site. Elements of contemporaneity and nostalgia informed the grafting of traditional materials onto a modernist aesthetic," David recalls. "That could have been what happened, but it wasn't. Conor got some of what he wanted, I got some of what I wanted and Nonda Katsalidis had to find a way to graft functionality and elegance onto the two big sheds that I had earlier foolishly foisted onto the site."

The brief was to provide a significantly larger winery than what was existing on-site, and increasing the facility capacity and barrel storage. Additional requirements were designing a wine bar, private dining and tasting spaces, and allowing a more public interface.

"What started with simply relocating the tank farm became a whole new project in its own right, when we considered the real aspirations and needs for the winery building," says Fender Katsalidis director, James Pearce.

Conor collaborated with the architects during the design process to ensure the aesthetics of the construction also met the additional winemaking challenges experienced at such a location. "Tasmania's weather changes so much and every vintage is so different from the last that we needed to find a way to work with that variability in the winery. Some years we have harvest over a long period, others are very compressed. We also have three vineyards, all of which take weeks to ripen one variety and need multiple harvests," he explains. "Everything from a production perspective was about trying to design a winery that could operationally achieve consistency out of variability. Essentially my request in design was to try to fit as much functionality and operational capacity as possible into a very small space. We managed to get three working levels and a gravity assisted winery out of it to help with both quality and sustainability," Conor concludes.

Key consideration was given to how the building would present itself visually, given it is prominently positioned on the estate, and provide a sense of destination to the museum's visitors. "We experimented with a number of tanks placed together and came up with a series of concave vertical forms, which provide a course of interesting shadows as the sun moves across the sky," James recalls.

With a limited footprint, excavations provided an underground cellar experience, and the wine bar is located to create a central meeting point for the village green and outdoor concert area. "The design of the building had to be interesting enough for it to be worthy of its siting on top of the hill, but not so extravagant that it's trying to overwhelm the site. The result is a self-assured and calm building, which contrasts intentionally with the underground gallery building," notes James.

Conor agrees: "By physically being in the centre of MONA and taking visual prominence on-site, I think the architecture helps tell the story of Moorilla. MONA is the main attraction, but it's hidden. Moorilla is more obvious as a structure, but one has to search to find the link on-site."

Describing his favourite part of the winery, Conor opts for "the feeling I have walking through it when everyone has left for the day. I find the space very comfortable and inspiring." As for David: "I like the bit inside the bottles."

Shaw Wines
Canberra

Canberra cool

A family-run estate on a prime elevated position within the cool climate region just north of Canberra, Shaw Wines began in 1998 when Graeme and Ann Shaw purchased Olleyville, an historic 280-hectare (700-acre) wool-making property dating back to the mid-nineteenth century.

Graeme and Ann continue to oversee operations while their two children, Tanya and Michael, and Tanya's husband, are full-time employees of a business that consistently produces a complete range of top-quality, estate-grown wines.

The fruits of their collective labours have resulted in more than 1,000 national and international medals and trophies, including the coveted title of Best Australian Cabernet Sauvignon from the London International Wine Challenge in 2018.

The family decided to build a new cellar door in late 2017 with the specific intention to "enhance the visitor experience to better enjoy our wines through different tasting spaces," according to business development manager, Karen Shaw. "The design vision had to take advantage of the rural vista and to make an immediate impression on visitors the moment they turned into our driveway."

Oztal Architects were approached by Graeme Shaw to be involved in the project, which had special significance to him and Shaw Wines. Prior to entering the wine industry, Graeme operated a successful building and development company that had worked with the architects on numerous projects.

Karen recalls the Shaws were "very aware of Oztal's capabilities and their ability to interpret the customer's design brief and nail it with the finished design."

The initial design concept was to create a building that could become a destination for wine lovers and improve the tourism potential for this local wine region. After co-habiting the site with a restaurant, the existing cellar door had lost its own identity – a problem the new building needed to address while offering a range of spaces that met the client's brief. The requirements were to be distinctive, take advantage of the views and offer patrons the opportunity to enjoy the experience of tasting wine without feeling like a retail space.

The resulting design is a bold building that reflects the quality of the wines produced in the vineyard and offers wine experiences in a range of spaces including an open seated tasting room, a relaxing wine lounge, and an exclusive private cellar. "The seated tasting area gives us the opportunity to present our wines in a more engaging way and showcases our amazing property in a more professional light," Karen states.

Nick Pelle, director at Oztal Architects notes: "The architecture offers a variety of opportunities for experiencing wine. Its space caters for groups and individuals and offers internal spaces with views and vistas of the vineyards … and wines are on display in various locations as a reminder of the products available."

A robust concrete wedge acts as a central spine to the building and defines the circulation space both linking and separating areas internally. It anchors the building and is expressed externally where it supports a butterfly roof structure that floats above the enclosure.

Internally there is a constant reminder and connection with wine, via vineyard views, the displays of signature wines and a highlight piece of sculpture – made of a collection of wine glasses – that filters light into the stairwell leading to the cellar below.

The tasting areas are transparent spaces that open up and reach out to the vineyards. Visitors can experience and explore the surrounding landscape and setting with vistas offering curated framed views that provide a connection between the raw material beyond and the finished product in their glass.

This transparency reflects the signature white wine produced by the Shaw vineyard. In contrast, the timber-clad entry exudes warmth and texture, is less revealing and thus more akin to a bottle of red wine, where the contents of the bottle are recognisable though not completely visible.

In overwhelmingly positive feedback from the client, Graeme told the architects that the combination of the building fabric and interior design meshed so well and, combined with the delivery of the construction, culminated in a building that exceeded his expectations and secured National Building Excellence awards.

Shaw Wines envisioned a cellar-door design that would be a 'must visit' regional destination for Canberra cool climate wines. "Our cellar door was designed to reflect this vision. The beauty of the concrete, wood, glass and steel combined with the vistas galore and award-winning wines makes us a destination to remember," according to the family. "There is no other winery in this region that offers the different levels of tasting experiences that we are able to at Shaw Wines."

The Overflow Estate 1895
Scenic Rim

Aligned with the vines

An unforgettable boutique winery boasting 12 kilometres (7.5 miles) of waterfront land on three sides, The Overflow Estate 1895 represents the culmination of a dream that began in 2006 when owner David Morgan visited a friend's bodega in northern Spain.

In the Scenic Rim region, on a peninsula on the edge of newly built Wyaralong dam, 60 kilometres (37 miles) south of Brisbane, the estate was established four years after David's inspiring European trip. Vineyards were planted using 2,500 vines chosen for their Mediterranean origins – each with a name, personality and place within this genuine home-grown estate – before the first vintage was harvested in January 2013.

Exceptional demand from locals, tourists and marketing agencies soon persuaded David and wife Noeleen of the need for a direct-to-customer cellar door that would pay respectful homage to the original namesake homestead, completed in 1895, for the then grazing property. They envisioned a barn that would blend with the grand homestead, the workshop, the machinery shed and stables while also providing something 'sharp, edgy, modern and exciting'.

The concept started as a tasting room and evolved into a brief that complemented the history and sat comfortably in its context. It was important to David that the structure aligned with the vineyard rows located a few metres away and blended with the natural environment.

Loucas Zahos Architects was approached to provide a cellar door for wine tasting and sales, capitalising on the increased tourism activity within the up-and-coming wine region. David had worked with Con Zahos previously and respected his 'brilliance, vision, warmth and cooperation' – important attributes for a complex design in a remote location.

The key architectural requirements were to design a facility that comprised a café-style tasting venue that encouraged customers to enjoy food and wine on the site surrounded by a large body of water. It needed to be of modest but relevant scale, in keeping with the specialist boutique approach.

"The materiality and form of this outdoor pavilion is a reference to the Australian agrarian shed. Used for storage of hay, equipment and machinery, these vernacular structures provide a pragmatic response to design. The design of the cellar door draws reference to this vocabulary," explains Con. The exposed structure of the steel-framed pavilion is composed of a series of metal-clad trusses that are aligned with the axis of the vineyard. These blades increase in height to support a simply pitched roof and reinforce the repetition of the rows of vines across the length of the open verandah.

This was part of the brief from the owner – to provide graceful and uninterrupted vistas to the lake and mountains.

Con notes that "cellar doors are often considered as annexes to vineyards where the primary function is the production and storage of wine. They often become a later add-on to the core activities of the winery." At The Overflow Estate 1895, however, the new cellar door is physically separate from the wine production and storage, but still provides a visual interaction between the two functions, which are integrated into a single building. "The architecture and materiality are industrial yet detailed and precise, a quality reflective of good winemaking. Today's wineries are more about social gathering … production and storage provide the framework for the destination to exist," Con says.

The wine-tasting experience promotes social interaction, relaxation and outlook to the surrounding landscape, whereas the winemaking requires enclosure, security and climate control.

The alignment of the building form is determined from the established vineyard rows, and while the wine-storage component is aligned with the source and concealed, the public space is transparent to the spaces around, providing for activity and connectivity to the water.

The expansive deck has magnificent views, and the colours and textures throughout have been selected to enhance the bush setting.

Architectural references to the Queensland vernacular are apparent in the large rainwater features and the verandah concept, which captures the breezes across the adjacent terrain and body of water. This provides for a unique experience compared to other wineries in the cooler southern climates throughout Australia. "It provides a stunning visual presence, a haven for peace and relaxation, limitless interesting glimpses of special design features, and an entrancing location for enjoying the award-winning wines and culinary creations," owner David proudly states. His only regret is that building hadn't happened sooner, as he describes his favourite part of the winery as greeting first-time visitors. "The looks of amazement, appreciation and pleasure are extraordinary. Imagine if they'd died without coming? What a tragedy," he modestly wonders.

Credits

Images have been reproduced with kind permission from the wineries, architects and designers with photographer credit as follows.

Amelia Park, Margaret River
Winery: Amelia Park Wines | ameliaparkwines.com.au
Architecture: Courtico Design + Architecture | courtico.com.au
Photography: Frances Andrijich (pp. 123, 124 top left, bottom) | andrijich.com.au; Tim Campbell (pp. 124 top right, 126–27) | timcampbellphoto.com

The Barossa Cellar, Barossa Valley
Winery: The Barossa Cellar | thebarossacellar.com.au
Architecture: JBG Architects | jbgarchitects.com
Photography: Dragan Radocaj (pp. 47–48); Hage Digital Productions (p. 49) | hagedigital.com.au; John Krüger | (pp. 50–51) | johnkruger.com.au

Barossa Valley Estate and Gardens, Barossa Valley
Winery: Barossa Valley Estate | barossavalleyestate.com
Architecture: DesignInc | designinc.com.au
Landscape design: Paul Bangay | paulbangay.com
Photography: David Sievers (pp. 53, 54–55, 57) | davidsievers.com

Beresford, McLaren Vale
Winery: Beresford Wines | beresfordwines.com.au
Architecture: Alexander Brown Architects | alexanderbrown.com.au
Interior design: Enoki Design | enoki.com.au
Photography: Beresford Estate (pp. 19, 24–25) | beresfordwines.com.au; Alyson Bagshaw (pp. 20–23)

Brokenwood, Hunter Valley
Winery: Brokenwood Wines | brokenwoodwines.com.au
Architecture: Villa + Villa | villaandvilla.com.au
Photography: Ross Coffey (pp. 91–93, 94 top left) | rosscoffey.com; Kevin Chamberlain (p. 94 top right) | kevinchamberlain.com.au; David Griffen (pp. 95 top right, 96–97) | davidgriffen.com

Clover Hill, Piper's River
Winery: Clover Hill Wines | cloverhillwines.com.au
Architecture: 6ty degrees | 6ty.com.au
Photography: Clover Hill Wines (pp. 231–34) | cloverhillwines.com.au

d'Arenberg Cube, McLaren Vale
Winery: d'Arenberg | darenberg.com.au
Architecture: ADS Architects | adsarchitects.com.au
Photography: d'Arenberg Winery (pp. 10–11, 13–16) | darenberg.com.au

Devil's Corner, Apslawn
Winery: Devil's Corner Winery | devilscorner.com.au
Architecture: Cumulus Studio | cumulus.studio
Photography: Tanja Milbourne (pp. 237–39, 241) | tmphoto.co

Domaine Chandon, Yarra Valley
Winery: Domaine Chandon Australia | chandon.com.au
Interior design: Foolscap Studio | foolscapstudio.com.au
Photography: Mike Emmett (p. 147) | redfishbluefish.com.au; Tom Blachford (pp. 148–49, 151) | tomblachford.com; Sharyn Cairns (pp. 152–53) | sharyncairns.com.au

Dowie Doole, McLaren Vale
Winery: Dowie Doole | dowiedoole.com
Architecture: Scholz Vinall | scolzvinall.com.au
Photography: James Knowler JKTP (pp. 27–31) | jktp.com.au

Hungerford Hill, Hunter Valley
Winery: Hungerford Hill | hungerfordhill.com.au
Architecture: Walter Barda Design | walterbardadesign.com.au
Photography: Justin Alexander (pp. 99–103) | justinalexander.com.au

Jackalope Hotel, Mornington Peninsula
Winery: Jackalope Hotel | jackalopehotels.com
Architecture: Carr | carr.net.au
Photography: Sharyn Cairns (pp. 185–89) | sharyncairns.com.au

Kimbolton, Langhorne Creek
Winery: Kimbolton Wines | kimboltonwines.com.au
Architecture: Damien Chwalisz Architects | damienchwalisz.com.au
Photography: John Montesi (pp. 85–87, 89) | johnmontesi.com

Leeuwin Estate, Margaret River
Winery: Leeuwin Estate | leeuwinestate.com.au
Architecture: Suzanne Hunt Architect | suzannehuntarchitect.com.au
Photography: Frances Andrijich (pp. 129, 130 top left, 132–33) | andrijich.com.au ; Jody D'Arcy (p. 130 top right, 131) | jodydarcy.com;

Leura Park, Bellarine Peninsula
Winery: Leura Park Estate | leuraparkestate.com.au
Architecture: Centrum Architects | centrumarchitects.com.au
Photography: Tatjana Plitt (pp. 227–29) | tatjanaplitt.com

Levantine Hill, Yarra Valley
Winery: Levantine Hill Estate | levantinehill.au
Architecture: Fender Katsalidis | fkaustralia.com
Photography: John Gollings (p. 155) | gollings.com.au; Earl Carter (pp. 156–57) | earlcarter.com.au; Shannon McGrath (p. 157) | shannonmcgrath.com; 4D Studio (pp. 158–59)

Logan, Mudgee
Winery: Logan | loganwines.com.au
Architecture: Stephen Buzacott
Photography: Logan (p. 117) | loganwines.com.au; Adrian Boddy (p. 118 top left, bottom and center) | adrianboddy.com; Kara Rosenlund (p. 119 bottom right) | kararosenlund.com; Jenna Kensey (pp. 120–21) | jennakensey.com.au

Medhurst, Yarra Valley
Winery: Medhurst Wines | medhurstwines.com.au
Architecture: Folk Architects | folkarchitects.com
Photography: Peter Bennetts (pp. 161–65) | peterbennetts.com

Mitchelton, Nagambie
Winery: Mitchelton | mitchelton.com.au
Interior design: Hecker Guthrie | heckerguthrie.com
Photography: Tom Blachford (pp. 221–23) | tomblachford.com; Simon Shiff (p. 225) | simonshiffsays.com

Mitolo, McLaren Vale
Winery: Mitolo Wines | mitolowines.com.au
Architecture: Tectvs Architects | tectvs.com
Photography: James Knowler JKTP (pp. 33–36, 38–39) | jktp.com.au; Mitolo (p. 37) | mitolowines.com.au

Montalto, Mornington Peninsula
Winery: Montalto | montalto.com.au
Architecture: Williams Boag Architects | williamsboag.com.au
Photography: Montalto (p. 191) | montalto.com.au; Tony Miller (pp. 192–93) | tonymiller.com.au; Regina Karon (p. 195, top) | karonphotography.com.au; Griffin Simm (p. 195, bottom) | griffinsimmphoto.com.au

Montoro, Orange
Winery: Montoro Wines | montorowines.com.au
Architecture: Source Architects | sourcearchitects.com.au
Photography: Tom Ferguson Ferguson (pp. 111–12, 114–15) | tomferguson.com.au

Moorilla at MONA, Hobart
Winery: Moorilla | moorilla.com.au
Architecture: Fender Katsalidis | fkaustralia.com + JAWS Architects | jawsarchitects.com + Rosevear Stephenson Architects | rosevearstephenson.com
Photography: Brett Boardman (p. 243) | brettboardman.com; Rémi Chauvin (pp. 2, 244) | remichauvin.com; Jesse Hunniford (pp. 245–47) | lusy.com.au

Oakridge, Yarra Valley
Winery: Oakridge Wines | oakridgewines.com.au
Architecture: Denton Corker Marshall | dentoncorkermarshall.com
Photography: Andrew Paoli (pp. 167–69) | paolismith.com.au; Oakridge (pp. 170–71) | oakridgewines.com.au

The Overflow Estate 1895, Scenic Rim
Winery: The Overflow Estate 1895 | theoverflowestate1895.com.au
Architecture: Loucas Zahos | loucaszahos.com.au
Photography: Christopher Frederick Jones (pp. 255–57) | cfjphoto.com.au; The Overflow Estate 1895 (pp. 258–59) | theoverflowestate1895.com.au

Passel Estate, Margaret River
Winery: Passel Estate | passelestate.com
Architecture: Theo Mathews Architect | theomathewsarchitect.com.au
Photography: Tim Campbell (pp. 135, 136 top left, bottom left and center) | timcampbellphoto.com; Photography Project (p. 137) | photographyproject.com.au; Kelly Harwood (pp. 138–39) | kellyharwoodphotography.com

Penfolds Magill Estate, Adelaide Hills
Winery: Penfolds | penfolds.com
Architecture: Denton Corker Marshall | dentoncorkermarshall.com
Photography: Colin Page (pp. 71–75) | colinpage.com; Peter Barnes (p. 76) | fotografo.com.au

Polperro, Mornington Peninsula
Winery: Polperro Wines | polperrowines.com.au
Interior design: Hecker Guthrie | heckerguthrie.com
Photography: Shannon McGrath (pp. 6, 197–99) | shannonmcgrath.com; Dom Cherry (pp. 200–201) | domcherryphotography.com

Port Phillip Estate, Mornington Peninsula
Winery: Port Phillip Estate | portphillipestate.com.au
Architecture: Wood Marsh Architecture | wood marsh.com.au
Photography: Earl Carter (pp. 203, 205–7) | earlcarter.com.au

Primo Estate, McLaren Vale
Winery: Primo Estate | primoestate.com.au
Architecture: Edwards Design
Interior design: Lisa Zamberlan
Photography: John Gollings (pp. 41–45) | gollings.com.au

Pt Leo Estate, Mornington Peninsula
Winery: Pt Leo Estate | ptleoestate.com.au
Architecture: Jolson | jolson.com.au
Photography: Lucas Allen (pp. 209–13) | lucasallen.com

Running Horse, Hunter Valley
Winery: Running Horse Wines | runninghorsewines.com
Architecture: Kaunitz Yeung Architecture | kaunitzyeung.com
Photography: Brett Boardman (pp. 105–109) | brettboardman.com

Seppeltsfield, Barossa Valley
Winery: Seppeltsfield Wines | seppeltsfield.com.au
Architecture: Max Pritchard Architect | maxpritchardarchitect.com.au
Photography: Dragan Radocaj (p. 59); Sam Noonan (pp. 60–63) | samnoonan.com.au

Shaw + Smith, Adelaide Hills
Winery: Shaw + Smith | shawandsmith.com
Architecture: JBG Architects | jbgarchitects.com
Interior design: Chris Connell Design | chrisconnell.com.au
Photography: David Sievers (pp. 79–81) | davidsievers.com; Jessica Clark (p. 82 top left) | jessicaclark.com.au; Shaw + Smith (p. 82 top right) | shawandsmith.com; Sean Fennessy (p. 83) | seanfennessy.com.au

Shaw Wines, Canberra
Winery: Shaw Wines | shawwines.com.au
Architecture: Oztal Architects | oztal.com.au
Photography: Shaw Wines (pp. 249–53) | shawwines.com.au

TarraWarra, Yarra Valley
Winery: TarraWarra Estate | tarrawarra.com.au
Architecture: Kerstin Thompson Architects | kerstinthompson.com
Photography: Derek Swalwell (pp. 5, 173, 175–77) | derekswalwell.com; John Gollings (p. 174) | gollings.com.au

Ten Minutes by Tractor, Mornington Peninsula
Winery: Ten Minutes by Tractor | tenminutesbytractor.com.au
Architecture: Cox Architecture | coxarchitecture.com.au
Photography: Katherine Jamison (p. 215) | katherinejamisonphotography.photodeck.com; Martin Spedding (p. 216 left and centre) | tenminutesbytractor.com.au; Jason Loucas (p. 217 right) | jasonloucas.com; Daniel Von Czarnecki (pp. 218–19) | danvon.com.au

Torbreck, Barossa Valley
Winery: Torbeck | torbreck.com
Architecture: JBG Architects | jbgarchitects.com
Photography: Pete Thornton (pp. 65–67, 68 top, 69) | whatpeteshot.com.au; Thomas Schaefer (p. 68 bottom) | unfilmed.net

Vasse Felix, Margaret River
Winery: Vasse Felix Wines | vassefelix.com.au
Architecture: Iredale Pedersen Hook | iredalepedersenhook.com
Interior design: Hecker Guthrie | heckerguthrie.com
Photography: Peter Bennetts (pp. 141–43) | peterbennetts.com; Frances Andrijich (p. 144) | andrijich.com.au

Yering Station, Yarra Valley
Winery: Yering Station | yering.com
Architecture: Conti Architects | contiarchitects.com.au
Photography: Ben Wrigley (pp. 179–80, 182–83) | benwrigley.com.au

Index

6ty degrees 235, 260

A

Aboriginal Art Association of Australia 224
Adelaide Hills region wineries 70–83
Adkins, Will 236
ADS Architects 12, 260
Age & Sydney Morning Herald Good Wine Guide, The 166
AIA, *see* Australian Institute of Architects, awards
Albert, Tony 90
Alcorso, Claudio 242
Alexander Brown Architects 18, 23, 260
Alternate Realities Museum 17
Amaout, Sam 98
Amelia Park 122–27, 260
Ando, Tadao 8
Apslawn region wineries 236–41
architects & designers 260–61, 267
   6ty degrees 235, 260
   ADS Architects 12, 260
   Alexander Brown Architects 18, 23, 260
   Ando, Tadao 8
   Ashton, Ted 220
   Bangay, Paul 56
   Bonato, Francesco 36, 37
   Botta, Mario 8
   Buzacott, Stephen 116, 119, 260
   Calatrava, Santiago 8
   Carr 184, 188, 260
   Centrum Architects 226, 229, 260
   Chapman Herbert Architects 43
   Chris Connell Design 78, 261
   Conti Architects 178, 181, 261
   Courtico Design + Architecture 122, 125, 260
   Cox Architecture 216, 261
   Cumulus Studio 236, 240, 260
   Damien Chwalisz Architects 84, 88, 260
   Denton Corker Marshall 70, 77, 166, 169, 261
   DesignInc 52, 56, 260
   Edwards Design 43, 44, 261
   Enoki Design 18, 260
   Fender Katsalidis 154, 157, 244, 260, 261
   Folk Architects 160, 164, 165, 260
   Foolscap Studio 146, 150, 260
   Foster + Partners 8
   Gehry, Frank 8
   Gillies, David 235
   Gomes-McNabb, Pascale 77
   Grounds, Roy 242
   Guthrie, Hamish 140, 145, 196, 199, 220, 224
   Hadid, Zaha 8
   Hassell Studio 210
   Hecker Guthrie 140, 145, 196, 199, 220, 224, 260, 261
   Iredale Pedersen Hook 140, 145, 261
   JAWS Architects 242
   JBG Architects 48, 64, 78, 260, 261
   Jolson Architecture & Interior Design 208, 210, 261
   Kaunitz Yeung Architecture 104, 261
   Kerstin Thompson Architects 172, 175, 261
   Loucas Zahos Architects 254, 261
   Marsh, Randall 202
   Max Pritchard Architect 62, 63, 261
   Ness, Patrick 216
   Nouvel, Jean 8
   Oztal Architects 248, 250, 261
   Pearce, James 247
   Pelle, Nick 250
   Piano, Renzo 8
   Portzamparc, Christian 8
   Rogers Stirk Harbour 8
   Rosevear Stephenson 242, 244, 261
   Rowe, Andrew 226, 229
   Scholz Vinali 26, 30, 31, 260
   Source Architects 110, 113, 260
   Stafford, Richard 52, 56
   Starck, Phillipe 8
   Suzanne Hunt Architect 128, 130, 260
   Tectvs Architects 36, 260
   Theo Mathews Architect 134, 261
   Villa + Villa 94, 260
   Walker, Peter 240
   Walter Barda Design 98, 103, 260
   Williams Boag Architects 190, 260
   Williams, Peter 190, 194
   Winteridge, Adèle 146, 150
   Wood Marsh Architects 202, 204, 205, 261
   Wood, Roger 202, 204, 205
   Zahos, Con 254, 256
   Zamberlan, Lisa 43, 261
Architectural Masterpieces of the Wine World 178
architecture, wineries, *see* architects & designers, wineries
art galleries, museums & sculpture parks
   Alternate Realities Museum 17
   Barossa Cellar, The 46
   Brokenwood 95
   Dalí exhibition, Salvadore 17
   d'Arenberg Cube 17
   Jackalope sculpture 188
   Leeuwin Estate 128, 131
   Mitchelton Gallery of Aboriginal Art, The 224
   Montalto 194
   Museum of Old and New Art (MONA) 244, 247
   Pt Leo Estate 208, 210
   TarraWarra Museum of Art 172
   Vasse Felix 140, 145
Ashton, Ted 220
Atlas, Ilana 166, 169
Australian Capital Territory, wineries in 248–53
Australian Institute of Architects (AIA) 37, 113, 175, 194, 205, 242
awards
   Architectural Masterpieces of the Wine World 178
   Architecture & Landscape award 84
   Australian Institute of Architects Awards 31, 113, 175, 194, 205, 242
   Australian Tourism Awards Hall of Fame 178
   Australian Wine List of the Year 210
   Australian Winery of the Year 166
   Best Australian Cabernet Sauvignon 248
   Best Winery Tourism Destination 194

Commercial Architecture 113
Global Best of Wine Tourism 58
Good Design Award 17
Good Food Guide 210
Gourmet Traveller Australia Hotel Guide awards 188
Great Wine Capitals Best of Wine Tourism Awards 84
Hotel, New Hotel and Regional Hotel of the Year 188
James Barnet Award 113
Keith Neighbour Award for Commercial Architecture 37
London International Wine Challenge 248
LUX International Hotel and Spa Awards 199
Most Relaxing Vineyard Stay 199
National Award for Commercial Architecture 205
National Award for Interior Architecture 205
National Building Excellence 251
NSW Country Division Awards 113
NSW State Architecture Award 113
Qantas Australian Tourism Awards 58
AIA South Australia Architecture Awards 31
Star Cellar Door Award 125
Victoria Chapter Commercial Chapter Award 175
Victorian Architecture Awards 205
Victorian Landscape Architecture Awards 210

B

Balthazar 69
Bangay, Paul 56
Barda, Walter 98, 103, 260
Barons of Barossa 46
Barossa Cellar, The 46–51, 260
Barossa Grape and Wine Association (BGWA) 46
Barossa Valley Estate and Gardens 52–57, 260
Barossa Valley region wineries 46–69
Beeston, John 90
Bellarine Peninsula region wineries 226–29
Beresford 18–25, 260
Besen, Eva & Marc 172
bin wines 70
Bonato, Francesco 36, 37
Botta, Mario 8

Boyd, Arthur 131
Boyd, Robin 220
Brokenback Ranges 90, 98
Brokenwood 90–97, 260
Broke Wine region 104
Brown Brothers 236
Brown Family Wine Group 236
BuildInc 23
Burgundy 172
Burke, Darren 226
Buzacott, Stephen 116, 119, 260

C

Cabernet Sauvignon 52, 90, 248
Calatrava, Santiago 8
Canberra region wineries 248–53
Carr 184, 188, 260
Case, Brad 84
cellar-door architecture, *see* architects & designers, wineries
Centrum Architects 226, 229, 260
Champagne 150, 181
Chandon Sunday School 150
Chapman Herbert Architects 43
Chardonnay 78, 116, 137, 172, 230
Château La Coste 8
Chris Connell Design 78, 261
Chwalisz, Damien 84, 88, 260
Clark, Nicole 84, 88
Clover Hill 230–35, 260
Constantine, Lloyd 140, 145
Conti Architects 178, 181, 261
cooking classes 229
Courtico Design + Architecture 122, 125, 260
Coverdale, Sam 196
Cox Architecture 216, 261
Cragg, Tony 210
Cricket Pitch Range 90
Crown Prince Frederick 230
Cru Bar + Pantry 95
Cube, d'Arenberg 12
Cudgegong River 119
Cullity, Tom 140
Cumulus Studio 236, 240, 260

D

D'Aloisio-Atlas family 166, 169
d'Arenberg Cube 12–17, 260
Delegat Group Limited of New Zealand 52
Denton Corker Marshall 70, 77, 166, 169, 261

Derrick, Bob & Jennifer 110, 113
designers, *see* architects & designers
DesignInc 52, 56, 260
design, wineries 8–9
Devil's Corner 236–41, 260
de Vogüé, Robert-Jean 146
Domaine Chandon 146–53, 26
Doole, Norm 26
Dowie Doole 26–31, 260
Dowie, Drew 26
Duke of Edinburgh 230
Dundon, Bronwyn & Rob 18

E

Edwards Design 43, 44, 261
E&E Black Pepper Shiraz 56
Enoki Design 18, 260
Ether Building, The 242

F

Fender, Karl 154, 156, 157
Fender Katsalidis 154, 157, 244, 260, 261
FINO (restaurant) 62
Floyd, Emily 188
Flying Brick Cider House 226
Folk Architects 160, 164, 165, 260
Foolscap Studio 146, 150, 260
Foster + Partners 8
Frederick, Crown Prince 230
Fromberg, David 104, 106
Furlong, Simone 128

G

galleries, *see* art galleries, museums & sculpture parks
G.A.M. Shiraz 32
Gandel family 208
Gehry, Frank 8
Gewürztraminer 116
Gillies, David 235
Gjergja family 202, 204
Gladigau, Jamie 48, 49, 64, 78
Goelet family 230
Gomes-McNabb, Pascale 77
Good Food Guide 210
Gordon, Daniela & Jeremy 122, 125
Gourmet Traveller magazine 63, 125, 194
Grange Cottage 77
Grange, Penfolds 70
grape varieties, *see* wines & grape varieties

Graveyard Vineyard 90
Graveyard Vineyard Shiraz 90
Great Wine Capitals Global Network 58
Grenache Shiraz Mourvèdre 52
Grilli family 40, 43, 44
Grounds, Roy 242
Guthrie, Hamish 140, 145, 196, 199, 220, 224

H

Hadid, Zaha 8
Halliday, James 90, 194
Halloran, Clare 172, 175
Hassell Studio 210
Hecker Guthrie 140, 145, 196, 199, 220, 224, 260, 261
Hobart region wineries 242–47
Horgan, Denis & Tricia 128
Hotel, New Hotel and Regional Hotel of the Year 188
Hungerford Hill 98–103, 260
Hunter Valley region wineries 90–109
Hunt, Suzie 128, 130, 131

I

ILR Reserve Semillon 90
Imperial 69
interior designers, see architects & designers
International Wine and Spirit Competition 178
Iredale Pedersen Hook 140, 145, 261

J

Jackalope Hotel 184–89, 260
Jack Rabbit Vineyard Restaurant 226
JAWS Architects 242
JBG Architects 48, 64, 78, 260, 261
Jolson Architecture & Interior Design 208, 210, 261
Jreissati, Elias 154
Jreissati, Samantha 157

K

Kalimna Bin 28 70
Kaunitz Yeung Architecture 104, 261
KAWS 210
Kerstin Thompson Architects 172, 175, 261
Kimbolton 84–89, 260
King, Inge 210
Kirby, James 98

L

Langhorne Creek region wineries 84–89
Langton's Classification of Australian wine 90
Leeuwin Estate 128–33, 260
Leura Park 226–29, 260
Levantine Hill 154–59, 260
Li, Louis 184
Logan 116–21, 260
Loucas Zahos Architects 254, 261

M

Margaret River region wineries 122–45
Marsh, Randall 202
Max Pritchard Architect 62, 63, 261
McLaren Vale region wineries 12–45
Medhurst 160–65, 260
Mitchell, John & Wendy 190, 194
Mitchelton 220–25, 260
Mitchelton Gallery of Aboriginal Art, The 224
Mitolo 32–39, 260
Mitolo, Frank 32, 36, 37
Möet Hennessy 146
Montalto 190–95, 260
Montoro 110–15, 260
Moorilla at MONA 242–47, 261
Morgan, David 254, 257
Mornington Peninsula region wineries 184–219
Most Relaxing Vineyard Stay 199
Mudgee region wineries 116–21
Muse 103
Museum of Old and New Art (MONA) 244, 247
museums, see art galleries, museums & sculpture parks

N

Nagambie region wineries 220–25
Napa Valley 169
Napa Valley estate 146
Ness, Patrick 216
New South Wales, wineries in
 Hunter Valley 90–109
 Mudgee 116–21
 Orange 110–15
Nolan, Sidney 131
Nouvel, Jean 8

O

Oakridge 166–71, 261
Olsen, John 131
One Broke Road 98
Orange region wineries 110–15
Orange Wine Week 110
Osborn, Chester 12, 17
Overflow Estate 1895, The 254–59, 261
Oztal Architects 248, 250, 261

P

Parr, Lenton 210
Passel Estate 134–39, 261
Pearce, James 247
Pelle, Nick 250
Penfolds Grange 70
Penfolds Magill Estate 70–77, 261
Petsinis, Christie 160, 165
Piano, Renzo 8
Pinot Gris 116
Pinot Meunier 230
Pinot Noir 78, 172, 230
Piper's River region wineries 230–35
Plensa, Jaume 210
Polperro 196–201, 261
Port Phillip Estate 202–7, 261
Portzamparc, Christian 8
Primo Estate 40–45
Princess Mary and Crown Prince Frederick 230
Pt Leo Estate 208–213, 261

Q

Queen Elizabeth II 230
Queensland, wineries in 254–59

R

Randall, Warren 58
Rathbone, Darren 178, 181
Riesling 78
Rigg, Iain 90
Rockey, George 210
Rock Paddock 30
Rogers Stirk Harbour 8
Rosevear Stephenson 242, 244, 261
Roseworthy Agricultural College 40
Rowe, Andrew 226, 229
Running Horse 104–9, 261
Ryan, Andrew 220, 224
Ryan, Gerry 220

S

Sauvignon Blanc 78
Scenic Rim region wineries 254–59
Scholz Vinali 26, 30, 31, 260
sculpture parks, *see* art galleries, museums & sculpture parks
Seppelt, Joseph Ernst 58
Seppeltsfield 58–63, 261
Sharp, David & Lyndsay 226, 229
Shaw + Smith 78–83, 261
Shaw Wines 248–53, 261
Shelmerdine, Ross 220
Shiraz 30, 52, 56, 70, 78, 90, 110
Source Architects 110, 113, 260
South Australia, wineries in
    Adelaide Hills 70–83
    Barossa Valley 46–69
    Langhorne Creek 84–89
    McLaren Vale 12–45
sparkling wine 146, 150, 230
Spedding, Martin 214, 216, 217
Stafford, Richard 52, 56
Starck, Phillipe 8
Steel, Simon 164
Stimpson, Barry & Wendy 134, 137
Sutherland, David & Sally 110, 113
Suzanne Hunt Architect 128, 130, 131, 260

T

TarraWarra 172–77, 261
Tasmania, wineries in
    Apslawn 236–41
    Hobart 242–47
    Piper's River 230–35
Tatachilla 26
Tectvs Architects 36, 260
Tempranillo 116
Ten Minutes by Tractor 214–19, 261
Theo Mathews Architect 134, 261
Thomas, Chris 26, 30, 31
Tighe, Timothy 98
Torbreck 64–69, 261
Torpy, Adam 230, 235

V

van der Reest, Conor 244, 247
Van Der Sommen, Michael 64, 69
Vasse Felix 140–145, 261
Vault, The 226, 229

Victoria, wineries in
    Bellarine Peninsula 226–29
    Mornington Peninsula 184–219
    Nagambie 220–25
    Yarra Valley 146–83
Villa + Villa 94, 260
Villa, Eduardo 94
vineyards, *see* wineries
vintners, *see* winemakers

W

Walker, Peter 240
Walsh, David 242, 244, 247
Walsh, Peter 122
Walter Barda Design 103, 98, 260
Warramate Hill 164
Western Australia, wineries in 122–45
Williams Boag Architects 190, 260
Williams, Peter 190, 194
Willunga Hills 17, 37
Wilson family 160, 164, 165
Wilyabrup Valley 125
wine & cooking classes 17, 46, 229
winemakers
    Albert, Tony 90
    Beeston, John 90
    Burke, Darren 226
    Case, Brad 84
    Clark, Nicole 84, 88
    Coverdale, Sam 196
    Derrick, Bob & Jennifer 110, 113
    de Vogüé, Robert-Jean 146
    Fromberg, David 104, 106
    Gandel family 208
    Gjergja family 202, 204
    Goelet family 230
    Gordon, Jeremy 122
    Grilli family 40, 43, 44
    Halliday, James 194
    Halloran, Clare 172, 175
    Horgan family 128, 130, 131
    Jreissati family 157
    Logan, Peter 116, 119
    Mitchell, John & Wendy 190, 194
    Mitolo, Frank 32, 36, 37
    Mondavi, Robert 128
    Morgan, David 254, 257
    Osborn, Chester 12, 17
    Randall, Warren 58
    Rathbone, Darren 178, 181
    Riggs, Iain 90
    Schubert, Max 70
    Shaw family 248, 250
    Shelmerdine, Ross 220

Spedding family 214, 216, 217
Steel, Simon 164
Stimpson, Barry & Wendy 134, 137
Thomas, Chris 26, 30, 31
van der Reest, Conor 244, 247
wine museums & galleries, *see* art galleries, museums & sculpture parks
wine regions, see also *wineries*
    Adelaide Hills 70–83
    Apslawn 236–41
    Barossa Valley 46–69
    Bellarine Peninsula 226–29
    Broke 104
    Canberra 248–53
    Hobart 242–47
    Hunter Valley 90–109
    Langhorne Creek 84–89
    Margaret River 122–45
    McLaren Vale 12–45
    Mornington Peninsula 184–219
    Mudgee 116–21
    Nagambie 220–25
    Orange 110–15
    Piper's River 230–35
    Scenic Rim 254–59
    Yarra Valley 146–83
wineries 260–61, 267
    Amelia Park 122–27, 260
    Australian Capital Territory 248–53
    Barossa Cellar, The 46–51, 260
    Barossa Valley Estate and Gardens 52–57, 260
    Beresford 18–25, 260
    Brokenwood 90–97, 260
    Clover Hill 230–35, 260
    d'Arenberg Cube 12–17, 260
    Devil's Corner 236–41, 260
    Domaine Chandon 146–53, 260
    Dowie Doole 26–31, 260
    Hungerford Hill 98–103, 260
    Jackalope Hotel 184–89, 260
    Kimbolton 84–89, 260
    Leeuwin Estate 128–33, 260
    Leura Park 226–29, 260
    Levantine Hill 154–59, 260
    Logan 116–21, 261
    Medhurst 160–65, 260
    Mitchelton 220–25, 260
    Mitolo 32–39, 260
    Montalto 190–95, 260
    Montoro 110–15, 260
    Moorilla at MONA 242–47, 261
    New South Wales 90–121
    Oakridge 166–171, 261
    Overflow Estate 1895, The 254–59, 261

wineries *cont.*
    Passel Estate 134–39, 261
    Penfolds Magill Estate 70–77, 261
    Polperro 196–201, 261
    Port Phillip Estate 202–7, 261
    Primo Estate 40–45, 261
    Pt Leo Estate 208–13, 261
    Queensland 254–59
    Running Horse 104–9, 261
    Seppeltsfield 58–63, 261
    Shaw + Smith 78–83, 261
    Shaw Wines 248–53, 261
    South Australia 12–89
    TarraWarra 172–177, 261
    Tasmania 230–247
    Ten Minutes by Tractor 214–19, 261
    Torbreck 64–69, 261
    Vasse Felix 140–45, 261
    Victoria 146–229
    Western Australia 122–45
    Yering Station 178–183, 261
wines & grape varieties
  bin wines 70
  Burgundy 172
  Cabernet Sauvignon 52, 90, 248
  Champagne 150, 181
  Chardonnay 78, 116, 137, 172, 230
  Cricket Pitch Range 90
  E&E Black Pepper Shiraz 56
  G.A.M. Shiraz 32
  Gewürztraminer 116
  Graveyard Vineyard Shiraz 90
  Grenache Shiraz Mourvèdre 52
  ILR Reserve Semillon 90
  Kalimna Bin 28 70
  Montoro Pepper Shiraz (2013) 110
  Penfolds Grange 70
  Pinot Gris 116
  Pinot Meunier 230
  Pinot Noir 78, 172, 230
  Riesling 78
  Rock Paddock 30
  Sauvignon Blanc 78
  Shiraz 30, 32, 52, 70, 78, 90, 110
  sparkling wine 146, 150, 230
  Tempranillo 116
Winteridge, Adèle 146, 150
Wiradjuri Aboriginal dialect 116
Wood Marsh Architects 202, 204, 205, 261
Wood Restaurant, The 95
Wood, Roger 202, 204, 205

Y

Yarra Valley region wineries 146–83
Yellow Rock 104
Yering Station 178–83, 261

Z

Zahos, Con 254, 256
Zamberlan, Lisa 43, 261

Acknowledgements

I am extremely grateful for the assistance, information and time generously provided by the winery owners and winemakers, and the architects and designers included in this book.

Wineries

Amelia Park: Daniela Gordon; Barossa Valley Estate and Gardens: Ryan Waples; Beresford: Keely Valente; Brokenwood: Krysten Barros, Iain Riggs; Clover Hill: Adam Torpy, Kiara Sullivan; d'Arenberg: Chester Osborn, Jack Scupham; Devil's Corner: Will Adkins; Domaine Chandon: Georgia Maddern; Dowie Doole: Olivia Brigden, Chris Thomas; Hungerford Hill: Bryan Currie, James Kirby, Steve Smith; Jackalope Hotel: Louis Li, Josh Ogilvie; Kimbolton: Nicole Clark, Penny Geue; Leeuwin Estate: Simone Furlong, Lucy Davis; Leura Park: Lyndsay Sharp; Levantine Hill: Melissa Jreissati, Samantha Jreissati; Logan: Peter Logan, Leigh Sargent; Medhurst: Simon Steel; Mitchelton: Andrew Ryan, Natalie Powell; Mitolo: Frank Mitolo, Kirsty Marie Mitolo; Montalto: John Mitchell, Susie Robinson at PR Darling; Montoro: Bob Derrick, Jennifer Derrick; Moorilla at MONA: David Walsh, Conor van der Reest, Alice Lewinsky; Oakridge: Tony D'Aloisio, Ilana Atlas, Stacey Fitzmaurice; Passel Estate: Wendy Stimpson, Barry Stimpson; Penfolds: Jess Minear; Polperro: Emma Phillips, Lori Hakim, Zarissa Shem; Port Philip Estate: Marco Gjergia, Melissa Gjergja; Primo Estate: Matteo Grilli; Pt Leo Estate: Serena Miszkowski; Running Horse: David Fromberg; Seppeltsfield: Nicole Hodgson; Shaw + Smith: Martin Shaw, Millie Haigh; Shaw Wines: Karen Shaw; TarraWarra: Clare Halloran, Kristy Williamson; Ten Minutes by Tractor: Martin Spedding, Gabby Richardson; The Barossa Cellar: Sally Collings, Louisa Rose; The Overflow Estate 1895: David Morgan; Torbreck: Michael Van Der Sommen; Vasse Felix: Lloyd Constantine, Kate Norman; Yering Station: Darren Rathbone, Vanessa Gasbarro

Architects and designers

Alexander Brown Architects: Alexander Brown, Brianne Mills; Carr: Aleesha Callahan; Centrum Architects: Andrew Rowe; Conti Architects: Robert Conti; Courtico Interior Design + Architecture: Beth Courtney; Cox Architecture: Patrick Ness; Cumulus Studio: Peter Walker; Damien Chwalisz Architects: Damien Chwalisz; Denton Corker Marshall: John Denton, Maria Giannakis; DesignInc: Kate Fitton, Richard Stafford; Edwards Design: Michael Edward Harvey, Bruce Watson; Fender Katsalidis: Karl Fender, James Pearce, Peta Michaelides; Folk Architects: Tim Wilson, Christie Petsinis; Foolscap Studio: Adèle Winteridge, Samuel McIntyre; Hecker Guthrie: Hamish Guthrie, Annabel Richardson; JBG Architects: Jamie Gladigau, Andrea van der Zande; Jolson Architecture & Interior Design: Stephen Jolson; Kaunitz Yeung Architecture: David Kaunitz; Kerstin Thompson Architects: Kerstin Thompson, Christina Souness; Loucas Zahos Architects: Con Zahos, George Hazell; Max Pritchard Architect: Max Pritchard; Oztal Architects: Nick Pelle, Dean Kensit; Rosevear Stephenson Architects: Craig Rosevear; Scholz Vinali: Oli Scholz; Source Architects: David Sutherland, Sally Sutherland; Stephen Buzacott Architect: Suzanne Hunt Architect: Suzie Hunt; Tectvs Architects: Francesco Bonato; Theo Mathews Architect; Villa + Villa: Maria Villa, Eduardo Villa; Walter Barda Design: Walter Barda; Williams Boag Architects: Peter Williams; Wood Marsh Architecture: Roger Wood; 6ty degrees: David Gillies; and Melany Wimpee Marketing and Communications Consultant for Jolson and Wood Marsh

A direct descendant of Jacob's Creek founder Johann Gramp, Alison Weavers (née Roennfeldt) is an architect with a career spanning 25 years in studios in Hong Kong, London and Sydney.

Alison's passion for architecture and wine has taken her to wineries around the world, from Bordeaux to Napa Valley, where she is as likely to admire the design of the venue as the drink in her glass.

She particularly appreciates how Australian winery design has evolved to create beautiful environments that complement and enhance the winemaking and wine-tasting processes. Alison has interviewed winery owners, winemakers, architects and designers to convey their stories about these exciting new wine destinations.

Published in Australia in 2021 by
The Images Publishing Group Pty Ltd
ABN 89 059 734 431

Offices

Melbourne
6 Bastow Place
Mulgrave, Victoria 3170
Australia
Tel: +61 3 9561 5544

New York
6 West 18th Street 4B
New York, NY 10011
United States
Tel: +1 212 645 1111

Shanghai
6F, Building C, 838 Guangji Road
Hongkou District, Shanghai 200434
China
Tel: +86 021 31260822

books@imagespublishing.com
www.imagespublishing.com

Text © Alison Weavers 2021 (Photographers as indicated in the Credits on pages 260–61. Endpapers: Amelia Park, Margaret River; Photography: Francis Andrijich.)
The Images Publishing Group Reference Number: 1603

All rights reserved. Apart from any fair dealing for the purposes of private study, research, criticism or review as permitted under the Copyright Act, no part of this publication may be reproduced, stored in a retrieval system or transmitted in any form by any means, electronic, mechanical, photocopying, recording or otherwise, without the written permission of the publisher.

 A catalogue record for this book is available from the National Library of Australia

Title: Through the Cellar Door: Australia's beautiful wineries and vineyards, their design and architecture // Alison Weavers
ISBN: 9781864709117

This title was commissioned in IMAGES' Melbourne office and produced as follows: *Art direction/production* Nicole Boehringer, *Senior editorial* Georgia (Gina) Tsarouhas, *Proofing* Jeanette Wall

Printed on 140gsm Golden Sun Woodfree paper by Artron Art (Group) Co., Ltd, in China

IMAGES has included on its website a page for special notices in relation to this and its other publications. Please visit www.imagespublishing.com

Every effort has been made to trace the original source of copyright material contained in this book. The publishers would be pleased to hear from copyright holders to rectify any errors or omissions.

The information and illustrations in this publication have been prepared and supplied by Alison Weavers and the participants. While all reasonable efforts have been made to ensure accuracy, the publishers do not, under any circumstances, accept responsibility for errors, omissions and representations express or implied.